The Ascensional Science of Spiritualizing Fruitarian Dietetics

Dr. Johnny Lovewisdom
1999

Paradisian Publications
in association with CreateSpace
San Francisco California USA
www.paradisianpublications.com

Disclaimer notice: The author and publisher are not responsible for any adverse effects or consequences occurring from the ideas, procedures or suggestions in this book. This book is not intended to replace the advice of a trained health professional. If you have a health problem you should consult a holistically and nutritionally inclined health professional.

First printing 2005

Copyright © 2005

All Rights Reserved

Reproduction or translation of any part of this work by any means, electronic or mechanical, including photocopying, beyond that permitted by the Copyright Law, without the permission of the publisher, is unlawful.

Printed in the United States of America

THE ASCENSIONAL SCIENCE OF SPIRITUALIZING FRUITARIAN DIETETICS
by Dr. Johnny Lovewisdom

After 25 million readers of the American weekly were informed he had been chosen as the Father of the New Race in 1942, in 1949 Doctor Johnny Lovewisdom was given renown described as a "Hermit" or "Saint of the Andes" to 100 million world-wide by the "Mundial" magazine of Montevideo "Picture Post" (G.B.) "Se" (Sweden) and numerous others in Europe.

"Only with the advent of the Paradisian New Race God-Born shall worth in my work be seen" Today 50 years later he continues as a Paradisian Essene still writing as a scientist about the Ascensional Science, and "Camp of Saints", after guiding top scientists to a "Sacred Valley of Longevity" at Vilcabamba, Ecuador and being viewed on T.V. since the 1960´s. As disciplinarian, he warns the world of Apocalyptic disasters starting before the end of 1999 and the New Age.

"IT IS THE SPIRIT THAT GIVES LIFE; THE BODY PROFITS NOTHING; THE WORDS WHICH I HAVE SPOKEN TO YOU ARE SPIRIT AND LIFE. BUT THERE ARE SOME OF YOU WHO DO NOT BELIEVE. I HAVE TOLD YOU THAT NO MAN CAN COME TO ME UNLESS IT IS GIVEN TO HIM BY MY FATHER." (John 6:63-65)

"Build paradise and eat the fruits thereof"

CONTENTS

MY CALLING TO THE CARPOPHAGOUS CONCEPTION   5

ELEMENTARY EVALUATIONS   6

GROWTH ENERGY FACTORS   10

ELEMENTARY EVALUATIONS PART II   17

RAPID EASY DIGESTION   19

IDEAL FRUITS LIST   22

PRIMATE'S DIET DIFFERENT THAN MAN'S   23

THE SECOND FORBIDDEN FOOD   30

SUGAR AND STARCH-FRIENDS OR FOES?   32

COLOR IN PROTEIN   39

TERTIARY ELEMENTARY EVALUATIONS   39

ALKALINE AND ACIDITY REACTIONS   39

ETHEREAL GASEOUS ELEMENT IN AMINO ACIDS THAT PROMOTE ASCENSION   41

AVOID A POISONED SOURCE OF CARPOPHAGOUS FOOD   54

GREEN PLANT CHLOROPHYLL CONCENTRATES RADIOACTIVE FALLOUT   55

THE FRUITARIAN MEDICAL DOCTOR   63

DR. HAUSHKA'S DISCOVERIES   66

HAUSCHKA, HERZEELE AND KERVRAN SHOW MAGNESIUM IS CHANGED INTO CALCIUM   71

GENESIS 1:29 CLARIFIED   75

WHY NOT AVOCADOS, OLIVES AND SEED OILS FOR SALADS?   80

APPENDIX: THE DIET OF JOHN   85

Publisher's note: Fruitarian or frugivorous means a fruit diet but includes fresh vegetables and grass-fed dairy products like cheese and yogurt. This is based on The Essene Gospel of Peace, The Healing God Spell of Saint John and El Evangelio de la Salud.

The Ascensional Science of Fruitarian Dietetics

MY CALLING TO THE CARPOPHAGOUS CONCEPTION

It was in 1936 after becoming a vegetarian due to my conscience against the killing of sentient beings for food, that I conceived the doctrine of eating only the palatable pulp covering of seeds that Nature intended to be food, which is defined as being Carpophagous. That year while engaged in picking strawberries in June, I carried on a debate seeking to convince a younger boy companion of my brother that he too should become a vegetarian like us. Altho a barren task as far as his conversion, it turned out to be very fruitful for me, because whatever good reason I could foster, he would answer with an imbecile innocence, saying, "But why", in his inability to give any counter-argument. So it was by these, "But whys", that led into my explaining that Nature is betrayed when man ingests the seed of plants, depriving them of their means of propagating their own species, as well as when we eat the roots, destroying their means of existence, beside whenever we consume the green leaves, which are needed for their growth, utilizing the carbon-dioxide that we eliminate and give us the oxygen we breathe to purify our blood, and produce the fruit we eat. This only leaves botanical fruits, or the palatable pulpy covering of the true fruits of trees and plants that Nature uses to beckon man to eat them, spreading the seed as well as when one eats berry seeds which are deposited hopefully in earth to give more of their kind. Live and let live is Nature´s First Law of Life for the intelligent beings designed in the image and likeness of God.

In two years I was living exclusively on juicy fruits, condemning the use of nuts in the fruit diet which other fruitarians before me had used with adverse results due to the lack of the life-giving living water in nuts, making them the Tempters of Satan. That the Living Food sent from Heaven of the Bible was the Palatable Jesus hanging from every fruit tree in the Manichean rendering of John´s gospel, I learned over a decade later in my study of Sacred Theology.

In the beginning on earth, God said, Behold I make every plant and every tree which yield seed for propagating its own kind: Fruit is for man´s food, and green herbage for the food of every sentient being that flies and moves upon the earth. (Modern Clarified version)

The Ascensional Science of Fruitarian Dietetics

ATTENTION

In the following treatise we shall be using the terms GROWTH ENERGY by which we will include any kind of tissue formation, which may be pathological in classification or considered benign usually, and what we define as SUBLIMAL ENERGY in contrast, referring to forces which upraise, elevate, levitate, ascend, spiritualize as well as which purify. Physical growth is gravitationally drawn to the grave of dead, earthy matter of man's physical composition, while spiritual or what we coin as sublimal growth is characterized by the ascendancy of spirit being born by and of God, into a heavenly or cosmic presence beyond a finite fixation, chemically, psychologically and spiritually. In turn, subliminal in psychology means below the threshold of consciousness or apprehension in contrast to our meaning of sublimal as being Superconscious or cosmically conscious, which is the original significative of translational, to translate, or to convey to heaven without death, as well as to enrapture or entrance, or sublime, joyful, elated or majestic, fitting for the Kingdom of Heaven. This work on Ascensional Science thus is dedicated to bringing these lofty ideals into the possible grasp of scientific minds, and yet across the threshold to abstract Divine or Cosmic Consciousness.

ELEMENTARY EVALUATIONS

In this unprecedented work of ultramundane pioneering sciences, we seek to find out just how the Paradisian beings lived and understood life for the 100 million years period that tree fruits have been cared for in prehistoric time. For the average human whose interest are served best with pornography, drug medications and economically profitable ventures all this will prove boring if not mentally aberrating. With this precaution, we shall proceed in the faith that the reader has had a glimpse into the way beyond life of deeper theology and fruitarian sublimal mentation. Fare thee well on the conquest of the Ultima Thule of my Hyperborean homeland, the region of sunshine and everlasting spring, where the inhabitants lived on juicy fruits, and knew not what suffering and death were. Shall we also overcome.

The Ascensional Science of Fruitarian Dietetics

In the precedent theses on Self-Realization of Buddhahood, and the Sublime Theology of the Heavenly Ecclesia of Essenes, we illustrated how thru deluding phenomena of inter-related continuity in Karma, or the concatenation of events gives rise to the universe without the need of a First Cause. Siddhartha Buddha showed all we are, shall be and have been is the result of our thinking. When the continuity of existence ceases in our minds, within our mind our madness shall clear of itself, and when our madness clears, Enlightenment is already present. For the essential nature of our Transcendental, Pure and Enlightened Mind is everywhere, permeating the phenomenal world. (Buddhist Bible) So abandoning antiquated anthropomorphic gods of the Hindus and Jews, we are released from the overwhelming burden of superstition and logically adopt the tenet of an Abstract God, which is Self-Realizable thru experience of abstract characteristics which need no other Enlightened Wisdom. We say Ascensional Science because Ascension speaks of the bodily ascent into heaven, and then fully clarify this by adding Spiritualizing Fruitarian Dietetics, because Spiritualize is defined as to make spiritual, or deprived of materiality, worldliness.

Flavius Josephus said John was deprived of the nature of humans because he lived like a spirit without a body. So his Gospel is about the Ascensional Science that spiritualizes. "No one has ascended to heaven, except he who came down from heaven, even the Son of Man, who is in heaven. As Moses lifted up the serpent in the wilderness, the Son of Man is ready for the Ascension." (Jn. 3:14) In the end he again says: "I go to prepare a place for you, and I will come again and take you to me, so where I am you may also be." (14:3) Altho added to the original, Mark 16:15 says that Jesus "Ascended to heaven and sat on the right hand of God", but the Acts clearly stated the Essene tenet: And when Jesus had spoken these things, "He ascended while they were looking at him a cloud received Him, and He was hidden from their sight." (1:9) We also quote Irenaeus and others say he remained even in Trajan's time (98-117 A.D.), so we feel John's Ascension was in 109. This is feasible because no one ever discovered John's grave, altho there is the grave of John the Presbyter, one of his contenders, and another of Cerinthus who published the Aramaic Gospel of John and the Apocalypse in Greek for European Christianity. Since John's Spiritual Birth was realized in his 29th year, from then a Buddha lifetime of 80 years was completed in 109 A.D., honoring Gautama for the tradition of designating him as Maitreya, Buddha after him.

The Ascensional Science of Fruitarian Dietetics

With this introduction from ancient scriptures, now we shall proceed to show that all this has a scientific basis in logic by our proposition of spiritualizing man, since worldly men live in a madness or psychopathy simply thru the observation of phenomena of an illusory concatenation of events in relation to the First Cause. All this shall pass away since it had no sense in beginning. All matter consists of positive and negative electrical charges in atoms invisible and inexistent except in theory.

In our courses (Vitalogical Hygiene page 72) we quote from Johannes Rutgers, M.D., a Dutch birth-control advocate, who held that sexual stimulation is produced by the consumption of spicy foods, and other stimulants, especially alcohol, all superfluous nourishment, especially of an albuminous nature, beside flesh eating. "Biologically, any kind of tissue formation, even if pathological (diseased), is the expression of a certain GROWTH ENERGY which must be present to produce the growth at all. When the reproductive cells have once been separated from their parent cells, they must be discharged from the body. The essential constituent of seminal fluid is a microscopic germ cell, in the harvest of an embryonic tumor. Even in regard to this discharge, the reproductive cells occupy a position between the increase of growth on one hand and the tumor on the other hand. Relief is experienced after the voiding of pus, so also sexually, desire is relieved every time reproductive cells are cast forth."

    Then we continue explaining how the embryonic tumor of trophoblast cells build a nest in the uterus, "The trophoblast cells dig right into the wall of the uterus, destroying uterine cells, taking nourishment from the blood and passing it on to sustain the first embryonic cells." From this briefing we see the blessing of human birth is nothing but the continuity of tumorous growth processes, the embryo into the fetus, and this into the human infant in the struggle of the fittest laws of the jungle. No wonder religion invented Virgin Birth of holy infants to console their followers. The innocent children we see are the concatenation of implanting tumorous growth in humans steeped in sin, sharing their diseased condition on a further road to degeneration and death. The Buddha and John lacked microscopes, and did not study germ cells much less practiced surgery, but they still could penetrate by insight into knowing what mortals suffer from one life into another.

    The pre-puberty youth we used to promote as the ideal in Vitarianism, was plainly erroneous in this perspective. As far as that goes our journal was named inappropriately since youth was not the ideal, really infantile, because it takes an octogenarian fruitarian to penetrate

The Ascensional Science of Fruitarian Dietetics

the series of errors that our fallen race has gotten into. As to the state of puberty in youth, the infantile tumor realizes metastasis. We use this term because childhood is a disease, a growth that is malignant, delinquent, due to the original sin, and adolescence makes metastasis possible. Metastasis is defined as a shifting of disease from one part of the body to another unrelated to it, as by transfer of pathogenic organisms or cells of a malignant tumor. No tumor is benign, not even a wart. So the metastasis of youth is the opposite of the Ecstasis of Everlasting Life. The malignant macrocosmic cell we call human has metastasized to engulf the whole living earth with overpopulation and ecological contamination now in death throes. What really our hands have gotten into is a mass of civilization, which medically speaking in its youth is a CANCER, precisely metastatic Cancer!

To gather perspective, let us analyze the Youth Paradigm of civilization. Where else should we find our hero than the ball park? Here we await the spectacle midst a crowd of people busy guzzling Coca Cola and devouring Hot Dogs and Hamburgers, if not ice cream. So this is the stuff American youth is made of. That ice cream making their mouth water turns out to be sugared hydrogenated fat, margarine, little removed from axle grease. That mass of ground up flesh in those buns is a pun of whether the butcher could really distinguish cancer cells from animal flesh as a result of animals fed cardboard, offal, fragmented grains far related from the chlorophyll-rich natural grass. The pun in the bun is its makings resembling the Styrofoam plates they sell tomatoes upon. In my first year at Juanita Grade School we learned, "What are little girls made of? Sugar and spice and all that´s nice; and What are little boys made of? Snaps and snails, and puppy dog tails!" Well, with such a fine education, learning to read and write the new language as we from foreign born parents from Finn Hill, told us just what those weaners were,- puppy dog tails since that is the only part of the dog like them if skinned, so as not to go into what weaners truly resemble. As to the stuffings of girls, that sugar biologically has less life or food value than a lump of clay. Spice? That must be the mustard.

After the first chapter, the Bible is the etiology of mankind´s disaster since the Fall in Genesis, and even Alex Carrel lamented man´s pathology as "biological sin".

Now our findings on the above mentioned "GROWTH ENERGY" can be measured with instruments that register the Mitogenic Rays of Gurwisch Kirlian photography, Rothen´s Enzyme Action at a distance, and Visual Micro-Observations of working enzymes as illustrated by Dr. Edward Howell. However "Growth Energy is the process of human infants, and identifies with tumorous growth found universally in animalistic forms of life, the short passing phenomena we mistakenly call life." The profound celestial purpose of "THE ASCENSIONAL SCIENCE OF SPIRITUALIZING FRUITARIAN DIETETICS" is to avoid or reject false pathological "Growth Energy" in our diets, just as we already have done with protein foods that sustain growth, and the seeds which are banks of growth energy awaiting to be sprouted. The use of sprouts with visible abuse of growth energy reserved for their own species, and not for voracious human tumorous parasites, can only build more of the same stuff.

Thus, we quote from the "Composition and Facts about Foods by Ford Heritage B.S.M.E. Researcher page 96 (we highly recommend obtaining a copy for reference) about Growth Energy Factors. Yet regardless to the author's intent, perhaps we found this exactly what our interest in "Growth Energy" Factors involves.

The Ascensional Science of Fruitarian Dietetics

Foods on which sun rays have a direct action on growth

FOOD	ENERGY	MINERALS
Watercress	114	18.0
Beet greens	106	22.0
Celery	97	16.9
Turnip greens	97	14.4
Mustard greens	93	13.3
Carrot tops	93	------
Kale	86	12.0
Lettuce	86	13.3
Parsley	86	14.7
Endive	81	16.6
Spinach	81	16.1
Dandelion greens	65	12.5
Alfalfa	52	------
Asparagus	45	7.2

FOODS GROWN IN GROUND

FOOD	ENERGY	MINERALS
Radish	88	14.5
Rhubarb	72	15.5
Turnip	54	8.1
Parsnip	45	7.2
Celeriac	41	8.6
Carrot	39	6.7
Yam	31	3.7
Horseradish	27	8.6
Potato	24	4.4
Garlic	21	3.7
Sugar beet	7	------

The Ascensional Science of Fruitarian Dietetics

Foods grown in the sun but the sun's rays have no direct action on growth.

FOOD	ENERGY	MINERALS
Tomato	54	7.7
Okra	49	7.2
Cranberry	57	1.6
Winter squash	54	5.3
Green Pepper	49	6.0
Eggplant	48	7.8
Lemon	47	3.1
Cauliflower	46	10.0
Irish moss	44	------
Common Cabbage	43	9.2
Sweet Red Pepper	43	5.3
Red Cabbage	41	7.0
Leek	41	6.1
Broccoli	40	10.0
Apricot	37	4.7
Pumpkin	36	9.5
Pimiento	36	------
Green beans	31	7.0
Peach	29	4.6
Jerusalem Artich.	28	8.8
Grapefruit	28	3.4
Whole wheat flour	24	------
Banana	23	3.3
Orange	20	3.3
Prune	19	2.6
Persimmon	17	2.5
Green pea	17	4.0
Fig	16	3.1

The Ascensional Science of Fruitarian Dietetics

FOOD	ENERGY	MINERALS
Apple	14	2.0
Lentil	12	3.4
Olive Oil	0	0
Vegetable Oil	0	0

There you have a Working Chart for determining Tumorous Growth Energy as we would class "Growth Energy" in childhood, youth and old age since all disease organisms are parasitical growths like tumors, and are the product of the body's own reproductive system (as a tumor) altho with a foreign life motivation, rather than Everlasting Life. Here Satan nudges me for listing under No Direct Action on Growth, -lentil, but since I never created the chart,- see you later, alligator.

The right-hand list of No Growth Energy radiation is of interest to Fruitarians. The lack of direct action on fruits makes fruits ideal for healing cancer and all tumorous growth of disease organisms. This gave Dr. Anna Brandt's "Grape Cure" such success, later promoted by Dr. Edmond Bordeaux Szekeley. Even carrots in juices gave better results than garden greens, while tomatoes and squash may even prove better, while fruits and their juices are the most popular healing regimen even promoted by ordinary medical doctors. In short Everlasting Life Energy is distinct from Tumorous Growth Energy. Briefer yet, Sublimal Potential is sought excluding Growth Potential. So in Paradise, the green herbs were for beasts and human infants needing growth energy, but reaching maturity, the Fruits were thus from the Tree of Everlasting Life and the Blood of the Son of Man was of Vine Fruits.

As to why the whole wheat, soybeans and lentils, like all seed food show so little Growth energy or life even, is due to the Inhibitor Enzymes, hiding the Growth Potential of a whole bank of enzymes springing into action when they are permitted to sprout. Adam and Eve may have been very sensitive to Sublimal Potential in fruits so as to avoid the poisonous ones, but picking almonds, pecans or mature coconut, the Growth Potential was hidden by dormancy, so they mistook the seeds to be harmless, letting Satan's strategy with edible seeds undo God's Everlasting Life Potential.

The botanic fruits such as squash, tomato, sweet pepper and eggplant are far better than the plant green leaves so high in oxalic acid

The Ascensional Science of Fruitarian Dietetics

and excessive alkalinity. The Ford Heritage lists on oxalic acid and alkalinity (page 66-68) also illustrate this point, and that by drying fruits the alkalinity can be brought up to coequal such greens. Thus, fruitarians must be wary about chlorophyll pushers who hold them back to at least use wheat grass or alfalfa, but chlorophyll denote a high magnesium content, true also of almond, soybean, cashew and Brazil nuts, peanuts and sesame seed, revealing false standards of the Forbidden Food Satan pushes.

Now, this leads to the flaw that we had to assume working with Dr. Herbert Shelton's and even Dr. Edward Howell's findings in our "VITALOGICAL HYGIENE". As Dr. Howell put it, "Enzymes emerge as a true yardstick of vitality", but this was with mental reservation in quoting Prof. Pearl of John Hopkins University who said, "The duration of life varies inversely with the rate of energy expenditure during its continuance." In short, the length of life depends inversely on the rate of living. This shows his "Enzyme Nutrition" assumes that "each child is born with a definite amount of enzyme potential", and has nothing to do with being God Begotten with Everlasting Life, unlike our text on the Law of Life in John's Gospel. When we wrote the National Enzyme Company for Dr. Howell's address, they wrote he died a number of years ago, and thus such theories have nothing to offer us.

Dr. Howell's remedy for activating growth rate in seeds did show how lettuce seed by sprouting was freed from growth inhibitors, the anti-enzymes, which were fully inactivated in 24 hours. In general the enzyme activity of sprouted seeds was at its height when the sprouts were one fourth of an inch long. This like a human embryo after its 3rd month of development, becoming the fetus proper in over 9 months gestation period. What this all comes to, is when the infant no longer is nourished inside its mothers body or from her breast, depending on outside sources, nevertheless the food sourced is not the fountain of Life Everlasting. This we know since it is concerned with the Growing Pains of Children, which now is brushed off by saying they are "Rheumatic pains that occur in children's muscles and joints", but originally were attributed to rapid growth. The rheumatic pains show an extremely grave sin in flesh eating beside grains and legumes, but the fundamental cause is Growth Accelerating Foods, which are even high in high alkalinity garden greens and carrots, turnips and potatoes. Fruitarian children are slower in growth and of greater endurance and longevity. People are taking in too much Growth Energy and growing disease organisms thus, when they are full grown in body, eating wrong.

The Ascensional Science of Fruitarian Dietics

What we are researching for is SUBLIMAL ENERGY, NOT GROWTH ENERGY, which comes with "-STAYING POWER", stability to realize the ETERNIZATION OF LIFE that our Paradisian ancestral heredity calls for.

The initiation of our studies into the Science of Immortal Life began in my Sophomore year in Kirkland High School in 1936 in Mr. Poage's Biology Class on my favorite thesis that we were born with the Potentiality of Immortal Life, based on the Best Seller work "Man, the Unknown" by Alexis Carrel, M.D., (1873-1944). He only achieved scarcely above the average length of life, and his study of a chicken's heart cell, most assuredly was not the source of Ever-Lasting Life! "Sophomore" by my beginning after 63 years at the same theme ought to bring forth a new Science of the same. The turning point was 57 years ago experiencing Divine Birth: transfigured into heavenly regeneration and my name inscribed on a Celestial Book of Life Everlasting, verified in the Apocalypse of John. It may still sound sophomoric, if you compare it to the born again Christians, but remember this was on a diet of capuli cherries,- a thing I saw in a clairvoyant vision in an Everglades Fruitarian Retreat where I had been living on tomatoes, oranges, grapefruit and watermelon. All these fruits have "No direct action Growth" in our list, and was predated with clairvoyant visions first in California, on to Florida and Pujili, Ecuador practicing fruitarianism.

What this proves as to a main guidance factor about sublimal energy, is that spiritual energy is found in botanic fruits. This includes the juicy fruits of trees and the fruits of the vine, including the melons, squashes, tomatoes, cucumbers, etc. and flowers like figs, broccoli and cauliflower. These fruits keep you in communion with Spirit and Truth. As long as the Elohim was in their presence, Adam and Eve lived right with birthright to Life Everlasting, but the day Satan broke the connection, they were cursed from that day they were to be dying, returning to the earth from which they were taken. Thus, they were given green herbage to eat till they return its elements to earth, but they even ate the seed grain in bread, until they repented after the birth of Seth, in exemplary eating of exclusively juicy fruits. This was a healthy rebellion against the waywardness of Seth's parents and brought them back to the original "PARADISIAN CONNECTION" that gives God-Communion of one's God-Begotten heritage.

Living in Quito in 1945 when fruits were not sprayed, I had every type of fruit to choose from and I also chose white cauliflower,

The Ascensional Science of Fruitarian Dietetics

remembering the fig blossoms I so relished in California, and even in the city I was super-psychic, sensing peoples thoughts. Likewise, in my first years at Shambhala Sanctuary using raw squash with papaya or bananas alternatively definitely proved itself with clairvoyant experiences. We are not referring to imagining things in the mind, but rather a brilliant techni-color cinerama experience contemplated by the single eye of the forehead, along with ordinarily what is not seen by others in ones surroundings, or far-off in the sky. Raw squash also gave the heroine in "Green Mansions" and other wilderness people clairvoyant and telepathic sensitivity. As soon as squashes are cooked their quality as fruit is lost, while their mineral content is not enough to cause growth, yet enough for staying power.

From the exposition we have abruptly brought upon our wayward path of the last 50 years, really in 1945 and 1949, we saw our need to burn our bridges,- with this erroneous path. NO longer are we seeking "Eternal Youth Life", inspired by sophomoric or infantile schemes and means. Now our Ascensional Science is concerned with Ever-Lasting-Life in our journal, ours being the "Paradisian School of Ever-Lasting-Life". Our goal is the restoration of the Paradisian Connection in mankind's heritage with super-conscious God-Birth. The Scripture teaches us how and we must listen for the Divine Calling and Experience it. In the coming lessons we shall give more charts on the Fruitarian Regimen. However, the "BUDDHIST ESSENE GOSPEL OF JESUS" Aramaic interpretations of your Christian Bible teachings are basic in unveiling the Truth. Come one, come all, to the Third Millennium Paradisian Throne of God!

Moreover we shall discover that Eve was so named "because she became Mother of all the Living Beings", all the animal kingdom in the biogenesis of Devolution that densely populated earth. Become ERUDITE IN CARPOPHAGOUS DIETETICS among the Prestigious Paradisians!

THE ASCENSIONAL SCIENCE OF SPIRITUALIZING FRUITARIAN DIETETICS ELEMENTARY EVALUATIONS PART II

"Yet who is doing sin is of the Adversary, for from the beginning is the Adversary sinning. (Genesis 3:4) For this was the Son of Mankind manifested, that He should be annulling the acts of the Adversary. EVERYONE WHO IS BEGOTTEN OF GOD IS NOT SINNING, FOR HIS SEED IS REMAINING IN HIM, AND HE IS NOT SINNING, FOR HE IS BEGOTTEN OF GOD. For this separates the children of God and the children of the Adversary. Everyone who is not doing righteousness is not of God, and who is not loving his brother; for this is the message you heard from the beginning, that you should be loving one another, not according as was Cain of the wicked one, and slays his brother... He who is not loving remains in death." (I-Jn.3:9-12,15) This we quote from John because it illustrates his Paradisian Paradigm, referring continually to Genesis or "In the Beginning", as to the word of God and the son of God. Thus Cain did not worship true God, because Yahweh is whom Cain dedicated his offerings, and Eve says she acquired Cain by Yahweh, showing that Yahweh is the Adversary God. In other words, Yahweh, the tribal God of the Jews, is the Adversary Spirit, who leads astray, which in Aramaic defines Satan by his characteristic, which the concordant Version interprets as "Adversary", just as God by John is Elohim, or the Father. In the concordant Version His seed refers to God´s seed, so that when His seed remains not in man, it is the seed of the Adversary.

Thus, Matthew gives the Essene explanation of not losing one's seed. "And there are eunuchs who emasculated themselves because of the kingdom of heaven. Who is able to contain it, let him contain it." (Mt.19:12) From this we get the word "Continence", absolutely containing the seed by self restraint. But why should one restrain from the loss of seed? Both Matthew and Luke elaborate on the subject. Luke (8:12,15) affirms, "THE SEED IS THE WISDOM OF GOD... Now that in ideal soil, these are they who are in their heart ideal and good, hearing the Wisdom of God are retaining it and are producing fruit with endurance." John taught his disciples to get into fruit production (15:16), and the Word is the "Wisdom" of God. So he alone teaches the means of attaining the Anointing Holy Spirit of the Living God, the meaning of Jesus Christ, which is the Wisdom and Seed, or the "Son of God" as well as of Man, the Ideal in Genesis 1:17 which the Elohim

The Ascensional Science of Fruitarian Dietetics

blessed as very good.

So what can Matthew add to this? "He who is sowing the ideal Seed is the son of Mankind. Now the field is the World. Now the Ideal Seed, these are the Sons of the Kingdom. Now the darnel are the seed of the wicked one. Now the enemy who sows them is the Adversary. The harvest is the end of the Eon. Now the reapers are the messengers." The Lamsa Aramaic Version, instead of darnel, Adversary, messengers and Eon, uses the words Tares, Satan, angels and world. Matthew also promises that he who is sown in ideal soils, who is hearing the Wisdom of god and understanding, is prospering in the Kingdom of heaven Mysteries as well as doing the will of God in fruit production. (Mt.13:38-39,23)

To coordinate this with what we said in the introduction to our Ascensional Science, we repeat in the Aramaic version; "NO MAN HAS ASCENDED TO HEAVEN, EXCEPT HE WHO CAME DOWN FROM HEAVEN, EVEN THE SON OF MAN WHO IS IN HEAVEN. JUST AS MOSES LIFTED UP THE SERPENT IN THE WILDERNESS SO THE SON OF MAN IS READY TO BE LIFTED UP. FOR GOD SO LOVED THE WORLD, THAT HE GAVE HIS ONLY BEGOTTEN SON, SO THAT WHOEVER BELIEVES IN HIM SHOULD NOT PERISH BUT HAVE EVERLASTING LIFE." Here John exhibits the Kundalini Serpent doctrine of Eastern Yoga which he studied at a Nepalese Buddhist monastery in earlier years putting it in Hebrew Aramaic terms or symbols. He tells us the son of Man is ready to be lifted up, so understanding His Word of Wisdom, your own Ascension begins this moment, in well thought out planning of your priorities in living. First in priority is that to be God-Begotten one must retain the Seed which is to have the Son of Man because lost seed is the seed of Satan, our Adversary. So sexual losses are produced from excess Growth energy, really Adversary Energy, and this we illustrate in the BUDDHIST ESSENE GOSPEL OF JESUS to be what is meant by turning the Jordan downflow into the Dead Sea, back to its source on Mt. Hermon. This takes place in the Natural Wilderness for the God-Encounter of hermits without worldly connections in the Paradisian Connection. This is the Second Coming when the Son takes us up with Him to Heaven.

The Ascensional Science of Fruitarian Dietetics

RAPID EASY DIGESTION

The next classification of ideal Fruitarian Dietetics is that of the importance of Rapid Easy Digestion. First we list the time in hours and minutes and which fruits and other foods comply to the time. MODERN LIVE JUICE THERAPY, written by your author in 1962, had this statement as to Fruit and Vegetable Juices: "Living liquids do not need much blood for their digestion. Solids demand large quantities of blood for their digestion, and when digestion fails, the life fluid of the body, the blood, no longer is produced from the foods eaten. It should be clear that the living liquids of the body can come from fluids and not solids. All solids end up in the toilet bowl. The reason why live juices accomplish such outstanding results in chronic and degenerative disease is because they do not consume large amounts of blood for their digestion, as is the case with solid foods which use more blood for their digestion than the weakened patients can provide. THE LIVING FRUIT AND VEGETABLE JUICES ALONE ARE ABSORBED BY THE BLOOD WITHIN 15 MINUTES AFTER INGESTION. In turn solids, such as the vegetables with their fibers, as well as flesh and grains require 4 to 6 hours for digestion preparatory to assimilation into the Blood. In fact the solids have caused the accumulation of impurities in the body's cells, if anything, and the liquids are the cleansers beside the restorers of living cells." Thus, the way to partake of hard solid fruits often called vegetables, altho botanically being fruits is reducing squash, pumpkin, etc. into living liquids or grating them finely. Eating such botanic fruits is not ideal but in cases it becomes necessary in lack of the ideal or with excessively sweet fruit.

1 hour 15 minutes: parsley.
1 hour 30 minutes: Sweet lemons (like tangerines), agar, and Irish moss.
1 hour 45 in.: Grapes, Raspberry, Mango, Olives, Avocado.
2 hours: Orange, Grapefruit, Sweet cherry, Tomato, Blueberry, raisin, Globe artichoke, beet greens, garlic, potato, brown rice.
2 hours 15 in.: Figs, Pineapple, Strawberry, Pear, cauliflower, carrot, asparagus, loose leaf, cos and iceberg lettuce.
2 hours 30 min.: Peach, Blackberry, Gooseberry, dried fig, leek, okra, dandelion greens, mushroom, almond, Lima bean, white rice.
2 hours 45 min.: Apple, Apricot, Currant, Watermelon, Summer squash, Plum, dried peach, beet, coconut, pecan, pignolia, wheat-bran.
3 hours: Banana, Guava, Sweet lime, Broccoli, Winter squash, Kohlra-

The Ascensional Science of Fruitarian Dietetics

bi, Common cabbage, Swiss chard, sweet corn, rhubarb, endive, dried prune, spinach, beechnut, filbert, lentil, white bean, wheat germ, soybean.

3 hours 15 min.: <u>Pomegranate, Casaba melon, Honeydew melon, Canteloupe</u>, cranberry, cucumber, sweet pepper, pumpkin, rutabaga, turnip greens, watercress, celery, onion, snap beans, radish, cashew nut, fresh pea, cowpea, millet, peanut, olive oil.

3 hours 30 min.: Eggplant, celeriac, mustard greens, parsnip, dried pea, rye grain, safflower and sesame seed, soybean oil.

3 hours 45 min.: <u>Persimmon, Quince</u>, red cabbage, barley, wheat grain.

4 hours: Brussels sprouts, turnip, horse radish.

We have not included the botanic fruits, nor the avocado or olive in the underlined ideal fruits. Likewise the dried fruits should always be soaked and not eaten as they are. Special combining must be made for botanic fruits and reduced proportions. For instance when I ate cauliflower raw with tomatoes, tiny seedling avocados were of one to 5 or more proportion, or 5 portions of squash, eggplant, cucumber in place of cauliflower. Avocados we have classified as passion-producing, akin to immature jelly coconut, green corn, etc. not suitable for healing menstruation and seminal losses. Cooking the squashes, pumpkin, broccoli, etc. does not digest them, because only raw foods contain their own digestive enzymes. Cooking destroys digestive enzymes, making the body re-synthesize necessary enzymes and consume large amounts of blood in their digestion. As Webster says pumpkin means "gourd or melon not eaten until ripe", classing it with melons. Our source for this chart seems far off classifying persimmons in a 3 hour 45 minutes category. Large California persimmons fully ripe we found to digest in about 2 hours, like most of the ideal fruits. Only one kind of fruit is best for digestion, combining slowing it up.

COMPOSITION OF <u>IDEAL FRUITS</u> IN 100 GRAMS OR PERCENT PORTIONS

FRUIT	WATER	PROTEIN	FATS	CARBOHYDRATE	CALORIES	ASH	DIGESTION TIME
APPLE unpared	84.4	.2	.61	4.0	5	.3	2 hr. 45 min.

The Ascensional Science of Fruitarian Dietetics

FRUIT	WATER	PROTEIN	FATS	CARBOHYDRATE	CALORIES	ASH	DIGESTION TIME
APRICOT	85.3	1.0	.2	12.8	51	.7	2 hr. 45 min.
CARISSA	80.8	.5	1.3	16.0	70	.4	na
CHERIMOYA	73.5	1.3	.4	24.0	94	.8	na
CHERRY sweet	80.4	1.3	.3	17.8	70	.6	2 hr.
sour	83.7	1.2	.3	14.5	58	.5	na
FIG	77.5	1.2	.3	20.3	80	.7	2 hr. 15 min.
GRAPEFRUIT	88.4	.5	.1	10.6	41	.4	2 hr.
GRAPES Amer.	81.6	1.3	1.3	15.7	69	.4	1 hr. 45 min.
European	81.4	.6	.3	17.3	67	.4	1 hr. 45 min.
LOQUAT	86.5	.4	.4	12.4	48	.5	na
MAMEY	86.2	.5	.5	12.5	51	.3	na
MANGO	81.7	.7	.4	16.8	66	.4	1 hr. 45 min.
CASABA	91.5	1.2	--	6.5	27	.8	3 hr. 15 min.
HONEY DEW	90.6	.8	.3	7.7	33	.6	3 hr. 15 min.
NECTARINE	81.8	.6	--	17.1	64	.5	na
ORANGE	86.0	1.0	.2	12.2	49	.6	na
PAPAYA	88.7	.6	.1	10.0	39	.6	na
PEACH	89.	.6	.1	9.7	38	.5	2hr. 30 min.
PEAR	83..2	.7	.4	15.3	61	.4	2 hr. 15 min.
PERSIMMON Kaki	78.6	.7	.4	19.7	77	.6	3 hr. 45 min.
Native	64.4	.8	.4	33.5	127	.8	3 hr. 45 min.
PINEAPPLE	85.3	.4	.2	13.7	52	.4	2 hr. 15 min.
PLUM Damson	81.1	.5	-	17.8	66	.6	2 hr. 15 min.
Japanese	86.6		.5	.12.3	48	.4	2 hr. 15 min.
Prune type	78.7	.8	.2	19.7	74	.6	2 hr. 15 min.

The Ascensional Science of Fruitarian Dietetics

FRUIT	WATER	PROTEIN	FATS	CARBOHYDRATE	CALORIES	ASH	DIGESTION TIME
POMEGRANATE	82.3	.5	.3	16.4	63	.5	3 hr. 15 min.
RASPBERRY							
Blk.	80.8	1.5	1.4	15.7	73	.6	1 hr. 45 min.
Red	84.2	1.2	.5	15.6	57	.5	1 hr.. 45 min.
SAPODILLA	76.1	.5	1.1	21.8	89	.5	na
SAPOTE	64.9	1.8	.6	31.6	125	1.1	na
SOURSOP	81.7	1.0	.3	16.3	65	.7	na
STRAWBERRY	89.8	.7	.5	8.4	37	.5	na
TANGERINE	87.0	.8	.2	11.6	46	.4	na
TOMATO	94.1	1.1	.2	4.7	22	.5	2 hr.
WATERMELON	92.6	.5	.2	6.4	26	.3	2 hr. 45 min.
BANANA							
Common	75.7	1.1	.2	22.2	85	.8	3 hr.
Red	74.4	1.2	.2	23.4	90	.8	na
Plantain	66.4	1.1	.4	31.4	119	.9	na
OLIVES							
Ascolano	80.8	1.1	13.8	2.6	12	2.5	1 hr. 45 min.
Mission	73.0	1.2	20.1	3.2	184	2.5	1 hr. 45 min.
Sevillano	84.4	1.1	9.5	2.7	93	2.3	1 hr. 45 min.
CAROB							
Pod	23.7	5.7	1.1	67.0	na	3.5	na
Flour	6.3	7.7	1.9	72.8	159	2.45	na

The above IDEAL FRUITS LIST, is followed beginning with Bananas then Olives and Carob, for the following reasons: Carob was used by John the Baptist, along with Bananas from Simon of Bethany's Banana Plantation. Bananas are the most popular fruit on earth available almost everywhere thru-out the year unlike seasonal fruits. Carob meal and bananas combine well, altho another juicy fruit is required for a liquid or living water balance. The Master Jain yogis of Mt. Abu India who live 1,200 years or more, fed mainly on figs, but sometimes ate olives, for which we judge they believed olives were health giving to balance the excessive sugar content of the figs.

The Ascensional Science of Fruitarian Dietetics

In our course VITALOGICAL HYGIENE we have proven that especially anatomically man is not adapted to carnivorous, omnivorous, and granivorous diets. Now, many have mistaken man to be equal to anthropoid primates in classification, which is fallacious. For instance, the Encyclopedia Britannica says more than 85% of the Gorillas diet is wild greens, plants and shoots, and no more than 15% and usually less is fruit. Its favorite food is wild celery, yet the gorilla weighs 500 lbs. The orangutan's diet is 50% green plants and 50% fruits. In the case of Gibbons 62% is fruit, while the Chimpanzee eats 67%, the most among primates. They eat wild celery, bedstraw, borage, thistles, nettles, bamboo shoots and prefer to eat banana plants rather than the ripe fruit. There are no nuts in their habitat, nor do they eat eggs, insects or small animals as some have theorized. However, all these primates continue devolving in the asphyxiating hot, humid tropical lowlands with high barometric pressure, continually coughing, with the nostrils dripping mucus and die like white naturists trying to adapt to the low tropics with pneumonia.

Yet, man is distinct even from such primates. The salivary glands of man secrete an abundant flow of alkaline saliva, containing diastase to convert the carbohydrates of fruits into dextrine. The saliva of the herbivorous animals is less alkaline and lacks diastase. Starch and sugar have to be converted into glucose and levulose before they can be assimilated. Greens being the natural food of the herbivorous contains practically no starch requiring no starch splitting diastase. Humans are a unique Frugivorous species as proven by their diastase or ptyalin.

The stomach of herbivorous animals is divided into 3 compartments, whereas the stomach of frugivorous beings is divided only into one compartment called the stomach proper, and then a smaller receptacle called the duodenum. It is the first section of the small intestines, or sort of an after thought perhaps, since man has strayed far from his fruitarian birthright. The various compartments of the herbivore stomach are complicated and adapted to the laborious digestion of grass, herbs and plants or even tree leaves which are rough fibrous food, yet rich in Growth Energy. But the main stomach as well as the duodenum of man are structurally and chemically adapted to the digestion of juicy fruits and vegetable juices. We have shown that most vegetables, such as turnip and mustard greens, red cabbage, brussels sprouts, watercress, radishes, snap beans, etc. take over 3 hours to digest, but if juiced, usually they digest in 15 minutes, showing that such energy and blood consuming vegetables are not the proper food of man as a frugivorous species who is born without juicers. Moreover, especially beet greens, celery, turnip and mustard greens similar to what the anthropoids relish, and which give them massive muscular bodies of 500 pounds adapted to survival in the jungle in sacrifice to having brain capacity and size of frugivorous humans. The small brain case bearing ridges over the eyes, across the back and down the center in the apes shows that when such beings devolved from humans living in tropical jungles, it was the chlorophyll rich green plants that stimulated them to overeat of difficult to digest food, producing enormous growth energy, sensual bestial reproductive power of their flesh. They went to the opposite extreme of God-like design of juicy fruit eating species conceived in the beginning by the Elohim and which God called blessed.

Man's intestines are inconvenient for the digestion of coarse raw fibrous grass and vegetables he has tried to adapt to. The herbivorous animals have intestines ten times the length of their bodies while the frugivorous humans are with the longest intestines of twelve times their body length, and the carnivore, omnivore and granivore require much shorter intestines. The longest intestines show the greatest efficiency getting the most possible, as well as special elements in the refined ripe fruit for man's mental and spiritual capacities at the summit of God's majesty on earth. The shorter herbivora, and even herbivora like the primates show the gross, coarse, fibrous and often toxic elements of green plants and tree leaves are to be eliminated rapidly. Well crushed nettles are not bad, but thistles, even in weeding require gloves, not to speak of eating them. The fact that the chimpanzee that eats the most fruits (67%) is superior in memory, learning ability and imagination, shows the exclusive fruitarian diet gives the partaker higher intellectual capacities if not extra-sensory perception. Man, according to biochemist Isaac Asimov, can absorb in the average human brain a million billion separate bits of information. How much better if he returns to a fruitarian diet.

Now, the human body is 60% water, 19% protein, 15% fat, 1% carbohydrate and 5% mineral. Then in comparative origins in turn the human brain is 81% water, 8.5% protein, 9.3% fat and 1.1% mineral. Human bones are water and fat free substances. In turn infants nourish from mother's milk, 87.7% water, 1.6% protein, 3.9% fat, 66 calories and .45% minerals. This is for humans who double their weight in 6 weeks, showing <u>excessive Growth Energy</u> for full grown adults.

In perspective to these facts, the human infant builds more BRAIN in a year than a cow in a lifetime, but the calf builds more bone

The Ascensional Science of Fruitarian Dietetics

in a year than cows in a lifetime. The gorilla weighs 500 lbs. but man on average weighs only 154 pounds. Hence the cows are bony structured, gorillas are muscular creatures and humans are brain pre-dominant. Now this relates to why milk proportions differ. Cow milk is 87% water, 3.5% protein, 3.7% fat, 67 calories and .7% ash. Goat milk is 87% water, 4.3% protein, 4.5% fat, 71 calories and .8% ash. Sheep milk is 80.7% water, 6.5% protein, 6.9% fat, 107 calories and .9% ash. Man builds brain, cows build bone and sheep, goats and cows have hooves and horns while the gorilla has muscle. The calcium and mineral ash is .7%, .8% and .9% in cows, goats and sheep milk which is twice .45% human milk ash. From this analysis one should be able to understand why man was frugivorous, cows, goats and sheep herbivorous and anthropoids half and half, frugivorous herbivora. This means man is meant to survive due to his brain powers, animals due to their bodily structure, altho up to now man has destroyed animals and his birthright to longevity, but the Paradisian New Race in the New Age will neither destroy other life, nor continue his reproduction of bone, muscle and epithelium for protection needs, but rather the more vaporous, ethereal, mental and spiritual features which are androgynous virgin born needing no sexual propagation, and this because they feed upon vaporous, ethereal substances in juicy fruits in preparation for heavenly ascension.

Next if you will note, when man devolved into primates, the greater Growth Energy of chlorophyll greens gave massive muscular frames in body, and also the hairier coarser skin covering built from the fiber combined with protein characteristic which comes in visible by the wool, horn and hooves of sheep with sheep milk having near twice the protein of cow's milk. The devolving of primates into other herbivora came with the excessive grass fiber. But as soon as coconuts became monkey's food, and monkeys devolved into squirrels eating nuts, you see the great dwarfing of body size due to the driest food substance lacking living water. Then with more calcareous seed substances and finally those from which man developed grains, gave rise to flying from tree to tree of flying squirrels, and from these to birds with an ability to fly up into the sky with feathers and wings, being the least massive in bodies in contrast to elephants, cattle and the primates, especially the gorilla which is almost entirely herbivorous. In the meanwhile, certain carnivorous beasts devolved when herbivora took to preying upon and eating the bodies of herbivora in new traits.

In Vitalogical Hygiene we showed that Epithelial Structure gave men kinky wool-like black hair, dark coarse skins of primates so

The Ascensional Science of Fruitarian Dietetics

as to devolve eventually into anthropoids. We are not ethically prejudice but only showing how animal kingdom traits devolved from humans, and man devolved from God. This is likewise evident from orange or golden fruits being the richest in the Anti-keratinizing Vitamin A which prevents epithelial growths in humans. Note how the people of the Andes who live on corn and barley almost exclusively were close to two feet shorter than the Scandinavians. However, with man´s recent tendency to omnivorous nutrition, he wonders why the population of the darker races is overwhelming with the white race dying out. It was Siddhartha Buddha who taught that the Idea of a Creator or First Cause is superfluous:- it is evident there could be no Creator since a creator thus still requires a cause, just like the First Cause. But beginning with Emptiness, the void, we have righteous cause for fulfillment, and all that is, was, and will be is the product of the thought conceptions we have had as to mankind, and as one God in the plural manifestation, as told of the Elohim who conceived heaven and earth.

Before our Ascensional Science, it was possible or prudent to deliberate on this aspect of the Godhead, since the Elohim were what is called the beginning by John, or OLaPh in Aramaic. Elohim is first used in the singular due to the singular verb in Genesis, but this Godhead becomes plural, because the Only Begotten (or first Begotten in the Lamsa version) became the ideal <u>God-Conceived Man</u> born of the same essence in Spirit, <u>bereft of matter</u>. Thus, as yet we have not made something from nothing. But John 3:13 says, "No man has ascended to heaven, except he who came down from heaven, even the son of Man who is in heaven." So the ideal God-conceived Son of Man returned ascending back to the Father in spirit, so there is both singular and plural since God´s Spirit cannot be divided. In John 14:3 he explains: "I go and will prepare a place for you, and I will come again, and take you to me: so where I am, you may also be." This means by returning to the Tree of Life, eating the juicy fruits, shall enable us to shed our materiality, becoming spiritualized or etherealized, so we may overcome and ascend to the Father. Thus, we realize "I and the Father are one," (Jn.10:30) since God´s Spirit is not divided against itself. As long as man lived in God´s Presence eating juicy fruits, he was one or in communion with god, but when the Adversary God Yahweh came, Satan lead man and woman astray. Thus wrong thinking, as the Buddha said, created this ill-conceived world of suffering.

Altho we have analyzed what men have found to be the weight of man´s bones, muscles, brain and body, and yet that is a pittance to

The Ascensional Science of Fruitarian Dietetics

the heaviest part of man. "Come to me, all you that labor, and are burdened and I will give you rest. Take up my Yoke (Cross) upon you, and learn from me, because I am meek and humble of heart, and you shall find rest for your souls. For my Yoke (Cross) is pleasant and my burden light." (Mt.11:28-30) In emphatic repetition we make sure you realize what this refers to: "Love not the world, neither the things that are in the world. If any man love the world, the love of the Father is not in him. For all that is in the world, the lust of the flesh, and the covetousness of the eyes, and the pride of material things, does not come from the Father, but is of the world" (I-Jn.2:3) So what buries mankind even before death, is the world under which he labors, struggles and eventually gets buried under, unable to ascend.

Let me give you an example of a beloved friend I had in California, who was a stone mason building rock houses and stone fireplaces, a fine fair Scandinavian with blue eyes and blond hair who worked bare chested without a hat saying the sun gave him energy in the desert heat 130 degrees F. giving him an exceptionally muscular body due to continually lifting the heavy stones and shaping them to fit in place. After a hard days work he would come home and his lovely wife who always sought to please him in every way, would have the dark pumpernickel bread with fresh butter, potatoes, vegetables, buttermilk and fruit ready for his supper beside tender love. But like in Eden, Satan astutely built the attachment, and after numerous years a dark, slim man came to love his wife at first sight, and suddenly she sought other advantages and told her husband he could leave, for she loved someone else now. Well my friend had built great attachment to her loving care but becoming a bachelor he could do nothing but think of the betrayal, and instead of beauty of mind and body, lifting heavy stones, cement and work tore down his body and crushed his spirit, so with all the healthy life before that he passed away in his sixties. We have noted in a similar way in Latin America people are very attached to marriage partners, brothers and sisters, children, parents and other family relations, beside what they own, their work and home area. The rest of the world, nations, religions and people in home town are competitors, easily disposed in enmity. This whole world is what we must forsake for God.

In turn a lady who was a model Paradise builder, and as a perfectionist she could never get along with any mate, sparse of friends and complained about artificial living and machines. But she got involved in mail order merchandizing selling natural products, and

The Ascensional Science of Fruitarian Dietetics

discovered how profitable it was to have a computer to make contacts world-wide to greet customers, and now her computer is an individual she can love beyond human limits like a god for her. The same is true for others whose life is centered around their television set. Not long ago it was radios, motorcycles or automobiles and before that periodicals.

Food and festivity also replaced man's loneliness, having lost his ecstatic life in oneness with his truly Beloved, the All Knowing Self and Everlasting Being. Then all such things become boring, scatter brained, like thousands of pictures on a movie screen giving the appearance of animated motion just like the composition of worldly illusion created by two lenses in the eye, the domain of Maya, Satan.

As you have witnessed there is nothing in the world that lifts man upward from gravity within him, so the 154 pounds of bone, fat, muscles, brain and digestive organs, swollen with excesses and disease are a burden rather than an asset, for they heap the whole world upon him. People quote the bible as they bury the dead saying that God will receive them in heaven, yet they don't understand what they are describing... It is our purpose in our Ascensional Science as a Spiritualizing Fruitarian Dietetics to show Theology can become a true Science, scientifically analyzing Nirvana or Ascension Everlasting in Life transmuting materiality into etherealized Spirituality.

Rarely can you find a person who anxiously awaits a whole night in rapturous meditation or contemplation in the freedom of Spirit. Even during the day it is possible to work at chores to maintain the upkeep of the body, yet mentally be absorbed in God's Presence uplifted in the Heavenly Realm.

Weeding the garden, picking fruit, irrigating, teaching, typing or writing as well as other activities need not take all one's attention or thought. Likewise, as to location you do not need to be living in the High Equatorial Andes to be protected from nuclear fallout with an organic fruit supply to be a fruitarian as we are doing at present. Even in Canada and Scandinavia fruitarianism is possible with foresight and resourcefulness.

You may be able to add a green house on the side or even roof of your home if not in your garden, and get earth where there is still humus 6 inches below the top surface soil now contaminated with fallout, beside using all organic fallout-free compost you can accumulate, and you will be able to grow an assortment of tomatoes, melons, if not tropical fruit as a strict fruitarian without radioactive fallout and

The Ascensional Science of Fruitarian Dietetics

chemical poisons. Being the work of you own hands, every mouthful will be satisfying and precious, unlike the poisoned or badly cared for produce on the market. No longer is there the feeling, "For you had your luxuries on earth, and have been greedy: you have fed your bodies as for the day of slaughter," (Heb.5:5) in pig-sty or hen house consciousness. Even as a Vitarian eating large bowls of kale, lettuce, and other growth energy foods, we were consuming chlorophyll-rich leaves like a geometric moth, a caterpillar larva that moves by alternatively advancing the front end of its body and bringing the rear in forward to form a loop, which thus is called a looper, inch or measuring worm. Put an end to your former "Looper Existence."

"Never sick, never die, Live like the Immortals!" That was my message in 1958 as a fruitarian living at El Inca north of Quito, just as it was in 1942 in Pujili, and already in 1938 when I left home, family relationships and inheritance in a wealthy nation. Even with such an origin on Finn Hill near Seattle we had fruits to eat all year around with many varieties of apples, pears, plums, currants, gooseberries, loganberries, raspberries, strawberries, grapes, etc. While I sat up in a black Tartarian cherry tree filling my belly, my mother would try to coax me to eat a cooked meal, but I would insist I was full and wanted nothing else. Many times I wandered off these ideals, but I have reiterated the majestic, super-rational wisdom in the God-Given Paradisian Plan for God-Evincing Beings, so let us quit our wandering.

Now, in your own mind as you wonder if I have given you the whole Truth, may I remind you that words cannot manifest it, only your own experience evinces it by emulation. So as told nearly 2,000 years ago, "Everything has been delivered to me by my Father, and no <u>one knows who the Son is but the Father;</u> and <u>who is the Father except the Son,</u> and <u>to whom the son will unveil Him</u>...O my Father, Lord of heaven and earth, because you did not hide these things from the wise and men of understanding and did reveal them to minors, yes my Father for it becomes a delight in your Presence". When Jesus' listeners asked what they should do to possess EVERLASTING LIFE, He told them to love the Lord with all their heart, mind, strength and intelligence and their neighbor as themselves, giving the example of who their neighbor is.

The Ascensional Science of Fruitarian Dietetics

THE SECOND FORBIDDEN FOOD FOR FRUITARIAN HUMANS

Not only did Genesis condemn as the Forbidden Food of Paradisians; the seeds of trees and plants, according to Spiritualizing Fruitarian Dietetics, and Vitarianism founded by Dr. Johnny Lovewisdom, but the Apostle Beloved of Christ, John, reincarnated condemns the eating of green chlorophyll-rich plants as the Second Sin From the Beginning, Genesis. In the face of world opposition, Dr. Lovewisdom has the pluck to defecate the oxygen-producing factories of plants on our planet from Spiritualizing Dietetics. The purist reasonability of this proposition evinces itself in the fact that chlorophyll in the presence of sunlight converts water and carbon-dioxide into carbohydrates, and in the process also produces the oxygen that humans and animals require for life. As a red-blooded believer and partaker of the blood of Jesus Christ in grape blood and fruit juices, I believe it is the acme of ingratitude that man should destroy green plants that produce the sugar, starch, fiber and consequent fat in animal life, and the air's oxygen that humans and animals breathe to replenish their blood's hemoglobin.

Mankind, in the face of ecological disaster has raped Nature of forests and green plant coverage of the surface land and polluted the lakes, seas and oceans destroying much of the marine vegetation. As Fruitarians, eating the unique God-Given Food of Man, it is nonsensical now to eat, not only the seed of plants which Nature intended for the propagation of their own species in trees and plants, but also the very leafage that produces the fruit sugar which makes fruits enjoyable. The word "fruit" comes from fructus in Latin, or enjoyment or a means of enjoyment. Yet steeped even more in sin, market fruits are picked green, unripe so as to be watery, sour, bitter or acrid, robbed of the true living enjoyability, making it necessary to artificially sugar them, in ruin of their wholesome vitality that God gave us in Paradise. Farmers and markets are disinterested in Paradisian welfare!

To enjoy fruit in its attractive golden, red or purple color, most exquisite fragrance and partake of the health giving goodness, nothing more than the warm sunshine of one's own garden, behooves the true Paradisian. The city smog belched forth by factories and the land-water-air transportation vehicles is asphyxiating mankind, unable to breathe, let alone enjoy the fruits of one's own Paradise. "Build Paradises and eat the fruits thereof," has been the Lovewisdom Message for time immemorial, plant their seed and maintain green our planet, keeping our true factories of life unlimited, free of the artificiality we misnamed civilization, progress, and what is nothing but the scientific destruction of life and people. Eve did enough as the Mother of all the living.

The biogenesis of the Devolution of Man into animals began with the anthropoids eating more and more on jungle herbage, abandoning the strictly frugivorous human fare developing muscular massive bodies due to the <u>Growth Energy</u> stored from chlorophyll, and from anthropoids came the herbivorous mammals with even more massive forms, but when animals turned to seeds and granivorous feeding, they dwarfed in size with the dryness and epithelial or keratin-forming substance giving feathers and wings, and along with these factors of disintegration, when beasts began to feed on one another, mammals took to the seas like whales, sharks and lesser fishes, finally ending up simplest life forms. All this started with man falling from his God-like Image in biogenesis from a Fruitarian, due to the Original Double Sin in Eden.

Very significant is the fact that when man lost his Paradisian Garden of enjoyable fruits that satisfy both thirst and hunger for living water and everlasting energy, he was given the very foods that produce thirst and growth energy that weigh earthy beings down with heavy bodies like beasts, to teach him a lesson as to what was wrong in violation of God's First Law of Life in Nature. "And you shall eat the green herbage of the field; in the sweat of your face shall you eat your bread, till you return to the earth from which it was taken, for earth you are, and to earth you are returning." (Gen.3:19) Fruits are water and carbon-dioxide which carbohydrates are photosynthesized from, that is gaseous elements that ascend up into the clouds of heaven from where the Son of Man descended, as John and other Gospels affirm. This was pure Ascensional Science full of very logical reasonability, but modern science bent on destroying man with killing power, wars against men.

The Ascensional Science of Fruitarian Dietetics

THE ASCENSIONAL SCIENCE OF SPIRITUALIZING FRUITARIAN DIETETICS
SECONDARY EVALUATIONS
SUGAR AND STARCH--FRIENDS OR FOES?

In the classification of foods in Fruitarian Dietetics we have come upon an interesting perspective, as to Vitamin A and Keratin Tissue. First let us observe Vitamin A is known by its absence, its stability in foods rests upon it being insoluble in water, but being soluble in fats, stable in heat, destroyed by drying, oxidation and very high temperatures. The effects of its deficiency are slow growth, poor bone and tooth development, night blindness, Keratosis and Xerophthalmia. International units per 100 grams are as follows: Carrot 11000, Kale leaf 10000, Sweet potato 8800, Turnip greens 8000, Beet greens 6100, Mango 4800, Sweet red pepper 4450, Winter squash 3700, Cantaloupe 3400, Japanese persimmons 2710, Broccoli 2500, Papaya 1750, Nectarine 1650, Carambola 1200, Tomato 900, Loquat 650, Watermelon 590, Tangerine 420, Sapote-summer squash 410, Red banana 400, Plum 190, Avocado 290; Guava 290, Cucumber 250, Mamey 230, Common banana 190, Globe artichoke 160, Red raspberry-Roseapple 130, Grapes 100, Fig-Grapefruit 80, Olive 60, Cauliflower-date-sapodilla 60, Pear-lemon-Kohlrabi 20, Cherimoya-soursop-lime-eggplant 10, Almond-coconut-white bean-barley-millet-rye-rice-wheat 0.

Noteworthy is the absence of Vitamin A in granivorous food and nuts, which made starches keratin tissue-forming seen mainly in granivorous birds, altho eating of herbage gave hair, horn, hooves along with massive bodies, while the golden fruits including squash and pumpkin (with 3700, 1600) are high in Vitamin A, well digested and allow bone development, growth, night vision keratinosis and xerophthalmia absence. Your editor lacked the ability to digest starches in high school having to be sans bread for lunch, and has tendency towards warts, malformation of nails, at 16 having 32 tooth cavities, osteoporosis and dandruff, all of which came by white bread, white sugar, pastry and cake served 6 times a day often with coffee among the Finnish colonists in his early ignorance of childhood. We had an abundance of green vegetables, beside berries and fruits, yet sugar and starch undermined my body's ability to utilize calcium and other minerals and expressed itself forming keratin tissue like deformed nails, acne, eye trouble, and above mentioned things. But the fact that most of the vegetables were canned or cooked at high temperatures, and some

The Ascensional Science of Fruitarian Dietetics

fruits, meant that the Vitamin A was ineffective. Likewise we rarely had citrus Bioflavonoids and the berries only a short season, allowing the lack of capillary permeability to nourish the teeth giving the many tooth caries.

However, this may be an oversight in Ford Heritage charts on Vitamin A because deficiencies do not tally. Hot red pepper dried have 77000 but only 21600 raw, almost three-fold increase of Vitamin A dried. Even more pronounced are Apricots when sliced oxidized and dried in the sun after sulfur ovened at 10000, but fresh they have only 1700 IU or 3.6. The Peach halves thus treated supposedly "destroying by drying, oxidation and very high temperatures" in one chart, in the Vitamin A chart show fresh peaches at 1330 IU near 3 times more dried at 3900. Pears have <u>3.5 increase by oxidation and drying.</u> However figs remain the same fresh or dried at 80 IU. Raisins are 20 IU but fresh are 100 IU Vitamin A, or <u>fivefold decrease by drying.</u> Are we to believe that sulfuring, dehydration and oxidation increase life and Vitamin A in apricots, peaches and pears, or that sun dried raisins lose life and Vitamin A potency. So-called dried figs are cooked in hot steam after dehydration, we learned living and working in the fruit industry in California and eating the fruits. Real dried figs falling in the grass under tree or picked to dry become hard as wood altho they resemble the fresh if when soaked in the winter, while steam-cooked figs taste cooked. In case of apricots dried without halving with their seed the result is not as tasty, but it is a sure thing the sulfur-ovened apricots do not have effective vitamin A or more life.

Now the Greeks named the pumpkin "pepon" meaning cooked by the sun, ripe, hence a gourd or melon not eaten until ripe. But the American Alogonquin Indians of Massachusetts, in turn called it "askootasquash" meaning eaten raw or uncooked. Thus we eat the zucchini and summer squashes in salads raw or immature and wonder if the Greeks had this vegetable.

While summer squash is thus a low starch or green vegetable. So our point is that starch in botanic fruits that others call vegetables is that they are an easy to digest type of starch. Dr. Edward Howell has established that "Nature has enclosed all raw food with correct and balanced food enzymes for their digestion".

Let us look at FOOD ENZYMES THAT DIGEST FOODS: APPLE peroxidase; BANANA amylase, maltase, sucrase; CABBAGE amylase; GRAPE peroxidase, poliphenoloxidase, catalase; MANGO peroxidase, catalase, phosphatase, dehydogenase; POTATO invertase;

The Ascensional Science of Fruitarian Dietetics

HONEY catalase amylase; RICE amalase; SOYBEAN oxidase, protease, urease; STRAWBERRY dehydrogenase; SUGAR CANE amylase, catalase, ereptase, invertase, maltase, oxidase, peroxidase, peptase, saccharase, trysinase. However wheat, rye, barley, corn, sweet potato, peanut, beside unripe mangos, papayas, bananas and other unripe fruit have enzyme-inhibitors that prevent digestion. So <u>the ENEMY is starchy food without enzymes action due to inhibitors, or cooking</u>, showing roots, tubers, grains, nuts and other seeds are wrong as food sources. Such foods have latent enzymes but yet they are useless, since nature put opposing inhibitors against their digestion to prevent man form eating them as an intelligent being. It is even worse cooking them, since thus both enzymes and enzymes inhibitors are destroyed; the body has to take over the task nature designed with doing naturally, having to resynthesize the needed enzymes to digest cooked. Raw squash, cauliflower, cucumber, artichokes, kohlrabi digest in two or three hours time, similar to cherries, figs, oranges, peaches, pineapple, tomatoes, various berries, apricots, apples, bananas and plums. Casaba and honeydew melons, pomegranates and persimmons all are said to take longer. Thus, I have illustrated the fallacious belief that starches in certain botanical fruits like cauliflower, kohlrabi, artichoke and various squashes do not digest raw, since to the contrary, nature put digestive enzymes in them to be digestible in same time as the ideal fruits. What makes ideal fruits ideal is the <u>pleasing sweetness,</u> which cauliflower, squashes, cucumbers and acid tomatoes lack. However, if one eats extremely sweet ideal fruit such as cherimoyas, bananas, sweet grapes, mangos, etc. often one desires tomatoes, kohlrabi, cauliflower, cucumber, etc. just to <u>balance the insipid sweetness.</u>

  The reason I make exception to teaching the ideal is because not everyone is living in their own Paradise with ideal fruits. Moreover, we are living in trying times, the market fruits are poisoned with sprays, preservatives, herbicides, chemical fertilizers, radioactive fallout, not to mention what could come soon. Eating raw botanic fruit organically grown will sustain your psychic intuitive faculties needed for survival, so God will guide you to the right solution. There is likely to be a complete cut-off from former assets, home, family, transportation and communications after the monetary values collapse due to inflation bankruptcy in economics, and thus without food in the cities there will be famine in the richest nations and their population centers, instead of the poorer undeveloped lands. Due to the past customs and habits of stimulating flesh foods and drink, not knowing how to satisfy their hunger, and without law enforcement and chaos in every field, people will be resorting to cannibalism, children dying from eating earth, just as happened here in South America and in Asia and Africa in the recent past due to disasters.

So when the hungry hordes loot peoples homes of all food, and all the machinery and conveniences are mere piles of metal and other material without electricity, gasoline or other energy source, and life becomes unbearable with constant searches and violence in the cites, it will be a happy alternative to flee to the mountains or other isolated region to start life all over independent of buying, selling and money. A simple cave, rock, log, adobe or natural material shelter and sackcloth if you are left without clothing, will have to do. Plant the botanical fruits, squash, melons, tomatoes, cauliflower, white or red heading cabbage for saeurkraut, etc. to give you the raw diet without fire, and artichokes, eggplant, kohlrabi and pumpkins are not things others are likely to ransack or steal, yet will keep nourished with living water foods. In the meantime people will learn to respect God´s Laws in order to survive and the cities shall disappear with the people working small plots of land growing their own food. They will eat figs, carob, olives, grapes, berries, apples etc. just as they did in paradise until they fell and began grinding and baking bread. You also in the meantime should have black and red raspberries, blackberries, strawberries, grape cuttings rooted or bearing, figs, apples, cherries, peaches, apricots, or if your climate allows it, subtropical or tropical ideal fruits, and other botanic fruits which produce in a short time of months from seed, which may provide you sustenance until the Ascension.

A greenhouse is ideal investment in the northern temperate zone especially, giving tomatoes, melons, cucumbers, or even tropical fruits if you have a source of heat from compost, wood or other lasting source. Those who survive will have intuitional Communion with the Omniscient Mind and live in the highest moral code not injuring a blade of grass like the Buddha and the Jains of Mt. Abu who endure millennial lives living on figs or other fruits exclusively.

As to 15 or more "B" Vitamins said to be essential for health, long living people ignored them instinctively. Adele Davis as an authority to such claims, suicided really eating so much liver, and other sources, so we shall postpone discussion on them until an advanced study of Carpophagous nutrition is presented. In turn, Vitamins A, C, D, E, etc. are factors coming with people living in a sunny climate on a fruitarian

The Ascensional Science of Fruitarian Dietetics

diet. The same is true of enzymes natural in fruits.

But let us observe briefly that such enzymes require in eggs, tributyrinase, lipase, phosphatase, peptidase, peroxidase, catalase, oxidase and amylase for digestion, but are destroyed by cooking to burden the body. To digest milk the chief ones are catalase, galactase, lactase, amylase, oleainase, peroxidase, dehydrogenase, phosphatase but there are actually 35 separate enzymes needed to digest milk, 30 of which are destroyed by pasteurization. White powdered milk, white flour, and white sugar at one time were thought to give man's food requirements. These white refined foods sent to famine stricken areas by wealthy nations, destroyed health and lives, so really they were sabotaging by poisoning the hungry to become rid of them, in their pretended philanthropy, and even now it has not improved.

Sugar cane requires amylase, catalase, ereptase, invertase, maltase, oxidase, peroxidase, peptase, saccharase, tryosinase, among 10 principal enzymes to digest it. Thus when one eats all the processed food-stuffs, one taxes the human body with the re-synthesizing dozens of plant enzymes, which overwhelms it in a short lifetime. This was one of my objectives in proving by abstinence in my 6 to 7 months fasts, since they are eating worthless trash like they send to famine victims. One would think the white race owed its color to the white in sugar, powdered milk and flour products, but when the black, brown, yellow and red races eat such anemic worthless food they remained the same color but unnaturally ailing like white people. Such people read the analysis of dried milk powder of the cartons, and in Quito I found people teaching children that bread and white flour products were rich in calcium necessary for sound teeth and bones, confusing the color of quick-lime, white refined food with white teeth and bones. It shows how multiple-factural knowledge, confuses by association and is filling the world with falsehood every year making past facts obsolete.

Now for those who question as to why we classify, in the Lack of Growth Energy Chart, the cabbage family of what otherwise are called vegetables only due to their use, but in botany are fruits, the word Cabbage comes from the Latin word "Caput" meaning head, and in Webster's dictionaries, in botany a head means a large compact bud, so the shape and color of the white head of cabbage, especially the Earliana variety, is identical to a white rose bud in miniature, before the rose hip is formed and if harvested early, it will give repeated heads, before sending up seed-pod tendrils. The Earliana is sweet, fine for eating with tomatoes, red peppers etc. as a fruit salad. In the case of drum-head cabbage there is no repetition of heads since the head is larger and late in the year, but the removal of the head enables immediate seed tendrils to come forth in tropical latitudes, or in the spring if the plant trunk with green leaves is protected from freezing. However, the cauliflower and broccoli are heads with obvious proof of being flowers, buds, blossoms, while the sweet pepper, eggplant, squashes, cucumbers, melons, tomatoes, etc. are self-evident as fruits. After this defense of the head cabbage as a white flower bud or blossom-fruit similar to the case of figs, the cauliflower and broccoli are unmistakably blossoms. By cutting the head, especially of broccoli, repeated heads are formed before the sending forth of seed tendrils. In the case of the white or purple sprouting broccoli, it resembles the tenderest cauliflower in taste and texture yielding nature's blessings which raw-foodists relish far more than the mushy soft mass of such things cooked. In the case of the kohlrabi, this was incorrectly named, not being or resembling a radish in any sense, much more resembling an apple eaten fresh from the plant, which we would prefer to call a "cabbage apple" or pomacol. They also repeat with smaller "apples", and avoiding injury to the green leaves on the trunk it will send up seed tendrils.

In the case of Brussels sprouts we feel they would be of dubious value as botanic fruits due to their difficulty of digestion, taking four hours. As to the purple eggplant with light lemon colored flesh it also is relished by raw-fooders, as are the mild sweet red peppers without question being nature's gift in unperverted flavors as true Botanic fruits, which can be combined with cauliflower, tomatoes, cucumbers and least of avocado or soaked dried olives. As to the sunflower tuber, called Jerusalem artichoke, it would seem controversial that it is not named as a "Growth Energy" food such as potatoes which are tubers. But tubers are not plant roots since you can harvest potatoes little by little and the plant continues growing like other produce of Botanic fruits. However, when we observe that potatoes have inhibitors preventing their digestion when eaten raw just as grains, legumes, nuts and other seeds, the reason is apparent why nature prevents us from eating them against her design. Jerusalem artichokes can be harvested continually without destroying its root and plant, yet the tuber does not warn us with anti-enzymes or digestion inhibitors. In the case of carrots that have no digestive inhibitors eaten raw, yet pulling up the carrot destroys the plant, visually repugnant to nature's law of live and let live. In the case of purple and globe artichokes, the harvest repeats giving forth

The Ascensional Science of Fruitarian Dietetics

fruit, and the base of blossom rejecting the fibrous petals, is with mineral of salty flavor balancing "Botanic Fruit Salads". Mentioning the salty flavor, I remember the "sea figs" growing around San Diego bay which were salty as sea dulse, but they also grew inland in California planted along the highways, better known as ice plants that yield a little fig shaped fruit with contents like a wild strawberry starting to dry but salty.

This leaves us only with green peas, okra and leeks in the list that prevents growths, which we care not to comment on not being ever fond of them raw. The enzyme inhibitors in grains, legumes, nuts and other seeds, in most roots and some tubers, beside the plants chlorophyll factories in the green leaves, if eaten cause destruction of life on earth, so let us live and let live, eating of "Botanic Fruits" now with measurable idealism toward perfection. The Buddhists and Jains of India were master-biochemists in not trodding on grass along a path in the perfection of the golden rule. This evaluation we make for those fruitarians who temporarily cannot have ideal fruits, as mentioned already having been driven from former homes in critical times of famine, etc. and yet it prevents being panicky in utter despair, going back to voracious eating of foods that are inferior or forbidden far from the ideal fruits or even the "Botanic Fruits". Hundreds of thousands have tried a fruit diet, especially among young people, but after a few months eating either poisoned market fruit or difficult to obtain ideal fruits, gave up, and went back to eating cooked foods, grains, animal flesh, taking stimulants, drugs, and many are resting under sod or suffering effects in disease and old age, and it is for them that we give a compromise but meaningful path to lasting results that cannot be regretted, in the everlasting Paradisian Connection.

The Ascensional Science of Fruitarian Dietetics

COLOR IN PROTEIN

To the other extreme from fruitarians who fear starch and avocado fat, when I lived in Vilcabamba in 1966, a fruitarian from Guayaquil came to see me due to his age and poor health. When I asked him what foods he ate he replied ordinary inexpensive fruits like oranges, papayas, mangos but rejected bananas as too sweet which your writer did living at such low tropical altitudes with barometric pressure that produces asphyxia, so that carbohydrates cannot be oxidized and the same is true of cherimoyas and other sweet fruit. It shows that sugar even of ideal fruits is more difficult to digest in tropical low altitudes, and because of this many idealists going to the tropics eating only fruit, after a few months are forced to go back to cooked starches, unable to stand sweet fruit. However, the man from Guayaquil, avoided going to cooked starches in his rare solution. He sliced plantains peeled green, and spread olive oil very lightly over them and placed them in the sun for half an hour before eating them. It was far from an ideal solution, but the raw white starch before ripening into sugar, became palatable with the oil showing raw starch more digestible than sugar in fruits when the barometric pressure prevents oxidation. However, the temporary solution did not last since in the long run nature cannot continue being deceived, so the anti-enzymes inhibiting digestion of the raw starch, even with oil brought on the man's crisis in poor health, due to trying to survive at such a low tropical altitude. The cooking of plantains or green bananas in place of roots is eaten in soup by poor people who can eat them free culled from shipping bananas for export from Guayaquil.

Next, it is also necessary to prefer some foods over others due to alkalinity in metabolic reactions in the body. The formation of a residue or ash results when the foods eaten are oxidized, thus relating to the above study of inhibition of oxidation in high barometric pressure. In this ash residue if the minerals sodium, potassium, calcium and magnesium predominate, over sulfur, phosphorous, chlorine and incombustible organic acid radicals, they are designated as alkaline ash foods. The opposite is true for foods described with acid ash high degrees of acidity and alkalinity.

ALKALINE AND ACIDITY REACTIONS

MOST ALKALINE: Cucumber 14.2, Avocado 10.7, Date 9.6, Granadilla 8.5, Tomato 8.3, Peach 8.2, Plum 8.2, Blackberry 7.7, Guava, Lemon 7.7, Cantelope 7.5, Loganberry 7.4, Sweet Cherry 7.3, Orange

The Ascensional Science of Fruitarian Dietetics

7.1, Prickly Pear 6.7, Apricot 6.6, Grapefruit 6.4, Nectarine 6.2, common Cabbage 6.2, Banana 6.0, Kohlrabi 6.0, Pineapple 5.8, Raspberry 5.7, Tangerine 5.7, Gooseberry 5.5, Mango 5.0, Quince 4.9, Sapodilla 4.8, Orange juice 4.5, Eggplant 4.5, Broccoli 4.2, Sour Red Cherry 4.1, Lemon juice 4.0, Red cabbage, 3.9, Pomegranate 3.5, Pear 3.4, Cauliflower 3.2, Pumpkin 3.2, Winter Squash 2.8, Grapes 2.7, Savoy Cabbage 2.7, Strawberry 2.6, Apple 2.2, Watermelon 2.2.
NEUTRAL REACTION GOING TO MOST ACID REACTION: Blueberry 1.4, Globe Artichoke 4.3, Jerusalem Artichoke 10.3.

We did not include dried fruits due to reasons already mentioned, and mention of citrus juices is to show that <u>juices give</u> a <u>more acid reaction</u> <u>than eating the whole fruit</u> chewing the fiber. Altho Almonds, Chestnut and coconut give alkaline reaction, Brazil nut, walnuts, lentil, peanuts, wheat, rye, rice and white beans give highly acid reaction. Soybean sprouts, green peas, green lima bean and fresh green corn are on the alkaline side.

The reason for some elderly individuals and even younger people sometimes doing better on fruits with a little starch content, rather than fruit sugar excesses, due to hypoglycemia, is because with a sudden rise of the blood sugar content due to rapid assimilation, they are <u>unable</u> to <u>oxidize</u> the <u>excess carbohydrates</u> causing untoward symptoms of nausea, lack of appetite, asphyxia, intestinal gas and indigestion. But the less sugary or sweet fruit with an acid balance, such as pineapple, orange, sour cherry and berries or with a slight starch content such as mealy apples or starchier cherimoyas, carob, summer squash, eggplant, kohlrabi, artichoke and cauliflower slow down the rate of metabolism, so there is an even, <u>gradual assimilation</u> of carbohydrates giving them staying power needed for the enduring life. Not only may there be asphyxia experienced at low altitudes in the tropics, but smoking tobacco or marijuana, or working in rooms filled with smoke, or cities with carbon monoxide from vehicular traffic, or near chemical industrial plants, even in the temperate zone one suffers from this suffocation.

The Ascensional Science of Fruitarian Dietetics

ETHEREAL GASEOUS ELEMENT IN AMINO ACIDS THAT PROMOTE ASCENSION

AMINO ACID MOLE. WT. ESSENTIALITY & FUNCTION FRUIT SOURCE

ALANINE $C_3H_7NO_2$ 89.09 ESSENTIAL Skin and Adrenal Glands Apples, Apricots, Orange, Grapes, Strawberry, Olive and Avocado (transitional), Cucumber

ARGININE $C_6H_{14}N_4O_2$ 174.20 ESSENTIAL Muscular contraction, Needs Pineapple or papaya to complete with most other fruits, Cartilage constituent, Control body cell degeneration reproductive organs

HISTIDINE $C_6H_9N_3O_2$ 155.16 ESSENTIAL Liver formation of glycogen, Mucus control, Hemoglobin and Semen Apple, Papaya, Pomegranate

HYDROXYPROLINE $C_5H_9NO_3$ 131.13 UNESSENTIAL Fat emulsifying, Formation of hematin and globulin in red blood corpuscles Apricot, Fig, Grapes, Cherry

IODOGORGOIC $C_9H_9NO_3I_2$ 433.92 UNESSENTIAL All glands, spleen, thyroid, pituitary, lymph, adrenals, etc. Pineapple, Tomato, Orange, Olive

ISOLEUCINE $C_6H_{13}NO_2$ 131.17 ESSENTIAL Regulation of thymus, spleen and pituatary, Hemoglobin, Regulation of metabolism Papaya, Banana, Tomato, Olive, Avocado, Broccoli, Cauliflower, Cabbage

LEUCINE $C_6H_{13}NO_2$ 131.17 ESSENTIAL Counterbalances Isoleucine Papaya, Banana, Tomato, Olive, Avocado, Broccoli, Cauliflower, Cabbage

The Ascensional Science of Fruitarian Dietetics

LYSINE $C_6H_{14}N_2O_2$ 146.19 ESSENTIAL Liver and gall bladder, Gut metabolism, Regulation of pineal & mammary glands, corpus luteus, oophoron, ovaries, Prevents cell degeneration Apple, Apricot, Grapes, Guava, Mango, Papaya, Pear, Orange, Banana, Tomato, Avocado, Cucumber, Cauliflower, Cabbage

METHIONINE $C_5H_{11}NO_2S$ 149.21 ESSENTIAL Contituent of hemoglobin, tissues, and serum, of spleen, pancreas and lymph Function Apple, Pineapple, Mango, Guava, Orange, Lime, Banana, Plantain, Tomato, Cauliflower, Cabbage

NORLEUCINE $C_6H_{13}NO_2$ 131.17 UNESSENTIAL Helps to balance Leucine functions

PHENYLALANINE 165.19 ESSENTIAL Involved in eliminating wastes, Kidney and bladder function Apple, pineapple, plantain, Banana, Tomato, Broccoli, Cauliflower, Cabbage

PROLINE $C_5H_9NO_2$ 115.13 UNESSENTIAL White corpuscles, Regulates emulsifying of fats Apricot, Cherry, Fig, Grapes, Orange, Olive, Pineapple, Avocado, Cucumber

SERINE $C_3H_7NO_3$ 105.09 UNESSENTIAL Tissue cleansing of mucous lungs and bronchial Apple, Pineapple, Papaya, Cucumber, Cabbage

THREONINE 119.12 ESSENTIAL Exchange of amino acids to establish balance Papaya, Banana, Plantain, Tomato, Broccoli, Cauliflower, Cabbage

The Ascensional Science of Fruitarian Dietetics

THYROXINE C15H1I4NO4 776.93 UNESSENTIAL Activity of throid, pituitary, adrenals, and orchic glands, Regulates metabolism & speed of reactions Pineapple, Tomato, Cucumber

TRYPTOPHANE C11H12N2O2 204.22 ESSENTIAL Generation of cells and and tissues, gastric and pancreatic juices, Optic system Guavas, Mango, Orange, Papaya, Pineapple, Banana, Plantain, Avocado, Tomato, Lime, Broccoli, Cauliflower, Cabbage, Cucumber, Squash

TYROSINE C9H1I4NO4 181.19 UNESSENTIAL Generation of red and white corpuscles, Active in Adrenals, pituitary, thyroid, hair Apple, Apricot, Cherry, Fig, Strawberry, Watermelon

VALINE C5H11NO2 117.15 ESSENTIAL Function of corpus luteus, mammary glands and ovaries Apple, Pomegranate, Banana, Plantian, Tomato, Squash, Broccoli, Cauliflower, Cucumber, Cabbage

The Ascensional Science of Fruitarian Dietetics

The above chart outlines the Body's need of Protein from outside source in the Ten Essential Amino Acids. From the Formula of these Amino Acids, we see that Essential ones are composed of Hydrogen, Oxygen, Nitrogen and Carbon Dioxide. Dioxide is the O2 radical in the formula denoting two atoms of the molecule are oxygen, and each molecule may have up to 14 atoms of hydrogen, 11 atoms of carbon, 4 atoms of nitrogen, and few exceptions have sulfur and iodine atoms. However, the latter sulphur and iodine factors raise the molecular weights up to 776.93, 240.30, 4433.92 which makes them objectionable for Ascensional Science which seeks freedom from earthly gravity. Carbon-dioxide is heavier than air and nitrogen forms four-fifths of the air, oxygen composing one fifth altho it is the most abundant element, while hydrogen is the lightest element that has the most Ascensional power. However, etherealness is not the only factor we need to consider since conscious direction with life and intelligence must coincide.

Our use of Ford Heritage, Rodale, and other sources in tables and charts, are not what their authors intended them for, but obviously Ascensional Science requires another new discipline, apart from Essential Amino Acids necessary for physical reproduction, nursing mothers, growing children, etc. The use and function in the body of the amino acids may be inaccurate, and the Botanic Fruits containing them also we selected biased for what guide-lines we work with now.

Thus, in the scheme of the next Chart seeking to relate Botanic Fruits to COLOR IN PROTEIN we shall first give the fruit, followed by what we considered most necessary minerals and vitamins, that is Calcium, Magnesium, Phosphorus, and Vitamin A. To avoid confusion in abbreviations of the colors, we shall use "V" for Verdurous or green, "G" for Golden or orange, "L" for Lemon, "R" for Red and "P" for Purple. In Purple we include what is called black (black fig) and "W" is for white.

The Ascensional Science of Fruitarian Dietetics

FRUIT	COLOR	PROTEIN	CALCIUM	MAGNESIUM	PHOSPHORUS	VITAMIN A
APPLE	W	.2	7	8	10	90
APRICOT	G	1.0	17	12	23	2700
AVOCADO (Calif.)	L	2.2	10	45	42	290
AVOCADO (Fla.)	L	1.3	10	45	42	290
BANANA Com.	W	1.1	8	33	26	190
BANANA red	R	1.2	10	33	18	400
BLACKBERRY	P	1.2	32	30	19	200
BLUEBERRY	P	.7	15	6	13	100
BREADFRUIT	W	1.7	33	-	32	40
CARAMBOLA		.7	4	-	17	1200
CARISSA		.5	-	-	-	40
CHERIMOYA	W-V	1.3	23	-	40	10
CHERRY sweet	P	1.3	22	-	19	1000
CHERRY Sour red		1.2	22	14	19	1000
CRANBERRY	R	.4	14	8	10	40
CURRANT Black	P	1.7	60	15	40	230
CURRANT Red	R	1.4	32	15	23	120
DATE	G	2.2	59	58	63	50
ELDERBERRY	P	2.6	38	-	28	600
FIG	P	1.2	35	20	22	80
GOOSEBERRY	G	.8	18	9	15	290

The Ascensional Science of Fruitarian Dietetics

FRUIT	COLOR	PROTEIN	CALCIUM	MAGNESIUM	PHOSPHORUS	VITAMIN A
GRANADILLA	G	2.2	13	29	64	700
GRAPEFRUIT	L	.5	16	12	16	80
GRAPES (American)		1.3	16	13	12	100
GRAPES (European)		.6	12	6	20	100
GROUND-CHERRY		1.9	9	-	40	720
GUAVA Common	R-L	.8	23	13	42	280
GUAVA Strawberry	R	1.0	23	-	42	90
JACKFRUIT		1.3	22	-	38	-
JUJUBE		1.2	29	-	37	40
KUMQUAT	G	.9	63	-	23	600
LEMON	L	1.1	26	-	16	20
LIME	L	.7	33	-	18	10
LOGANBERRY	P	1.0	35	25	17	200
LOQUAT	G	.4	20	-	36	670
LICHEE		.9	8	-	42	-
MAMEY	G	.5	11	-	11	230
MANGO	G	.7	10	18	13	4800
CANTELOUPE	G	.7	14	16	16	3400
CASABA	W-L	1.2	14	-	16	40
HONEYDEW Muskmelons		.8	14	-	16	40
NECTARINE	G & W	.6	4	13	24	1650
OLIVES Ascolano		1.1	84	-	16	60

The Ascensional Science of Fruitarian Dietetics

FRUIT	COLOR	PROTEIN	CALCIUM	MAGNESIUM	PHOSPHORUS	VITAMIN A
OLIVES Mission		1.2	106	-	17	70
OLIVES Sevillano		1.1	74	-	20	60
ORANGE	G	1.0	41	11	20	200
PAPAYA	G	.6	20		16	1750
PEACH	G&W	.6	9	10	19	1330
PEAR	W-L	.7	8	7	11	20
PERSIMMON Kaki	G	.7	6	8	26	2710
PERSIMMON Native	G	.8	27	-	26	-
PINEAPPLE	W & G	.4	17	13	8	70
PLANTAIN	R	1.1	7	--	30	-
PLUM Damson		.5	18	9	17	300
PLUM Japanese		.5	12	9	18	250
PLUM Prune-type	G-P	.8	12	9	18	300
POMEGRANATE	R	.5	3	-	8	-
PRICKLY PEAR	R & W	.5	20	-	28	60
RASPBERRY Black	P	1.5	30	30	22	-
RASPBERRY Red	R	1.2	22	20	22	130
ROSE-APPLE	L	.6	29	-	16	130
SAPODILLA	G	.5	21	-	12	60

The Ascensional Science of Fruitarian Dietetics

FRUIT	COLOR	PROTEIN	CALCIUM	MAGNESIUM	PHOSPHORUS	VITAMIN A
SAPOTE	W & G	1.8	39	-	28	410
SOURSOP	W-G	1.0	14	-	27	10
SUGARAPPLE		1.8	22	-	41	10
TAMARIND	R	2.8	74	-	113	30
TANGERINE	G	.8	40	-	18	420
WATERMELON	R	.5	7	8	10	590

NON- IDEAL FRUITS

FRUIT	COLOR	PROTEIN	CALCIUM	MAGNESIUM	PHOSPHORUS	VITAMIN A
ARTICHOKE Globe	V	2.9	51	-	88	160
ARTICHOKE Jerusalem		2.3	14	11	78	20
BROCCOLI	V	3.6	103	24	78	2500
CAULI-FLOWER	W	2.7	25	24	56	60
CHAYOTE	W	.6	13	-	26	20
CUCUMBER	W- V	.9	25	11	27	250
EGGPLANT	L -P	1.2	12	16	26	10
KOHLRABI	W	2.0	41	37	51	20
PEPPER Sweet Green		1.2	9	18	22	420
PEPPER Sweet Red		1.4	13	-	30	4450
PUMPKIN	G	1.0	21	12	44	1600
SQUASH Summer	L	1.1	28	16	29	410
SQUASH Winter	G	1.4	22	17	38	3700
TOMATO Red	R	1.1	13	14	27	900
CAROB St. John's Bread		5.7	-	--	-	-
CAROB FLOUR	G	7.75	22	95	1	227

The Ascensional Science of Fruitarian Dietetics

There may be numerous surprises in store for you, especially in the high quantity of Vitamin A in certain golden fruits, which prevent keratin tissue formation-hair, hooves and horn. No wonder mythology depicts the devil with horns, hooves and hair in particular places, beside the tail. It vouches for the Botanical Fruits associated with starch content as to being digestible without evil effect eaten uncooked, as is the case with winter squash, pumpkin, sweet peppers and broccoli. It pushes the esteem of the tomato and cucumber up, and especially the sweet fruits such as the watermelon, tangerine, sapodilla, various plums, roseapple, persimmon, peach, orange, papaya, plantain, nectarine, canteloupe, mango, mamey, lichee, loquat, loganberry, kumquat, guava, granadilla, gooseberry, elderberry, black currants, sour red cherries, carambola, blackberry, red banana, avocado and apricot. However, the ground cherry called "husk-tomato" which I grew by the crater-lake Quilotoa, is quickest of Vitamin A fruits to produce along with watermelon and cantaloupe, while the mango is queen among them all. Liquefy bananas with berries to digest bananas better.

Many fruits may have a rich store of minerals in the skin when ripened soft, such as bananas, papayas and oranges may be peeled thin of outer orange coating with inflammable oils leaving the white inner part very rich in Bioflavinoids and calcium. Apples that are low in vitamin A with the skin have over twice the Vitamin A to pared apples. Eating oversweet kinds of cherries reduces the vitamin A nine-fold. As to dissolving tumorous growth and disease organisms beside keratin tissue this is most effectively done by protein digesting enzymes such as found in papayas, pineapples, figs and our experience with raw unheated squash, especially the zambo of the Andes region, beside the single seeded chayote. In "Vitalogical Hygiene" we give "Elixir of Immortality" milk shake, which combined the chayote with col de monte juice which we thought to be excellent. We particularly suspect the chlorophyll of green leaves now as being another factor in producing sexual passion and seminal and menstrual losses, beside the protein and seed foods. Due to the leaf protein in green foliage now promoted as a high-grade protein, it seems likely that is the other guilty factor, since all the giant beasts become so prolific eating chlorophyll-rich grass and reproduce like rabbits.

If you wonder what our color in Protein conclusions may be, we state Verdurous is adverse in all green leaves. It is good in the green skin of white fruits such as some kinds of apples, cherimoya, soursop, beside botanic fruits like broccoli and globe artichoke. Lemon is ideal

The Ascensional Science of Fruitarian Dietetics

grapefruit, yellow grapes, roseapple, casaba melon, eggplant and some summer squashes. Golden Orange is ideal in oranges, papayas, apricots, peaches, persimmons, etc. Red is ideal in the tomato, watermelon, strawberry and pomegranate. Purple is ideal in black figs, black raspberry, purple grapes, loganberry, blueberry, purple cabbage and purple broccoli. White is plentiful. VERDUROUS thus gives harmony and stability. LEMON Yellow is cooling, calming to nerve energy, GOLDEN Orange is spiritualizing intelligence and warmth of compassion. RED is life-giving vitality and pureness of blood. PURPLE is for spiritual devotion and moral integrity. WHITE is for the totality of color, the complete color, the spiritual purity of white light.

In 1938 visiting spiritual centers in California we went to see Mr. and Mrs. Kulgrenat Atascadero who published the "Beacon Light" magazine. For 27 years they had been vegetarians promoting the Essene cause and had an orchard producing organic apples, of which we enjoyed apple juice which they served us, yet when we arrived their idealism had vanished going back to cooked meat-eating omnivorism. However, we noticed the light yellow clearness of the rapidly juiced apples. But later working at an apple ranch and cider mill, we witnessed the near brown color of the apple cider they sold, showing a great degree of oxidation. Thus, the apple eaten whole without oxidation have 8 mg. per 100 g. portion of Magnesium, showing the whole apple had twice the magnesium that the juice does, and probably very much less in the brown oxidized cider, causing gas and other symptoms.

Now, it is significant to note that Magnesium may be fairly well found in the golden fruits rich in vitamin A, with the anti-keratin tissue forming factor. This shows that <u>nature intended that mature seeds, roots and the green foliage are not the food for mankind,</u> as we showed in our Elementary Evaluations as to Growth Energy. Now, better than going back to eating sprouts of seeds, this vindicates the eating of immature fresh green peas, fresh immature corn, jelly coconut and the green beans that the Chart favors therein. To illustrate my point the green soybean Vitamin A content is 690 IU while when sprouted it is only 80 IU, equal to the dry mature soybean. So eating immature peas, snap beans, corn etc. is better for stability or lasting energy in the older persons, but to the contrary, must definitely be avoided as Passion-Producing Foods in people suffering form seminal and menstrual losses, just as one does avocados and coconut in such individuals. Also it is noted that eating soybean sprouts causes a decaying stench in the people unlike the fresh immature legumes.

The Ascensional Science of Fruitarian Dietetics

Thus our publisher in India, Dr. J.D. Narula included green peas as a staple in a predominately juicy fruit diet, enabling him to live 115 years tending to illustrate staying or lasting stability. Likewise the green soybean has 225 mg. phosphorous, as compared to 67 mg. seen in the sprouts, showing the immature ones possibly to be a brain food for intellectuals, altho younger folk engaged in sports or heavier work find such brain food counter-productive, because they give sexual losses. Since older people and people tending to be born eunuchs have a background achieving more stability staying power or able to last longer especially beyond 60 to a century or more, they no longer have sexual losses, and their bodies are able to metabolize the immature green peas, corn or okra in the lasting energy list (without growth energy), without overdoing and instead favoring the living water foods that cleanse the organism. It is like feeding when a person is ill, in that the food nourishes disease organisms rather than make one strong. Young individuals tend to be of immature emotions, unsure of themselves, going to extremes, as I have witnessed by hundreds going on most ideal fruits for a few months, and with the slightest adversity, jump back to habitual ways, concluding that fruits are not a good or practical diet. We tell you of raw foods, not so ideal temporarily, but back to habit or worse often, hoping you will strive to better others by your example even using botanical fruits in trying circumstances.

OUR RULE OF GUIDANCE is to stay whenever you can with ideal fruits, avoiding dates, bananas, cherimoyas and oversweet fruit because rare individuals, those with high metabolism get sexual losses from them, as well as avocados, etc. already mentioned since they can give excesses of growth energy, because THE LIVING WATER CONTENT OF FOOD IS THE LEADING BENEFICIAL FACTOR. And nature has designed some of its botanical fruits with a high living water content to help you in determining the beneficial ones.

The living water in cucumbers is 95%, in summer squash is 94%, in ripe tomatoes is 94.1%, in water melon is 92.6% and in eggplant is 92.4%, qualifying them as the fruit of the vine and living water that the New Testament Scriptures emphasizes.

The only fruit named as existing in the garden of Eden is figs, either true figs, or "Musa Paradisiaca" as bananas are called in Asia, Palestine and Arabia, since Adam and Eve clothed themselves in fig leaves, and thus some Apocryphal Scriptures say the figs were then the

The Ascensional Science of Fruitarian Dietetics

size of watermelons, showing that watermelons date back to Eden in the inference, so this tends to illustrate that the wise Patriarchs were able to live near a millennium of age living on figs and watermelon. In confirmation of this the Master Jain biochemists lived on figs and rarely olives which fell in the dry grass under the tree, and then stored till winter or spring, they can be soaked giving a food resembling fresh fruit more than other such dehydrated fruits.

In turn we have told of John the Baptist eating carob meal cakes moistened with bananas mashed and Jesus multiplied the fig loaves, which are dried figs pressed into what was the popular "bread" of the poor all over the Mediterranean area. Figs have existed millions of years while Paradisian man lived on and produced fruits, but grains have only existed 10,000 years, and grains for baked bread are too costly in labor to produce, while figs even today are the staple of the poor. Carob meal has 95 mg. of magnesium while bananas have 33 mg., but in turn carob has 227 IU of Vitamin A to common banana Vitamin A being 190 IU, or preferably red bananas with 400 IU of Vitamin A. Botanic Fruits are not for those who want millennium longevity.

Finally, we come to the mystery of Jesus squeezing grape blood into a chalice at the Eucharistic Supper for the Apostle at Easter in the Spring, when it is too early for fresh grapes, and seeming late to have autumn grapes. Yet, the Apostles could have realized this also for the occasion, since it is a fine old art today forgotten due to modern cold storage, in which if purple fall grapes are taken gently without bruising, harvested by large branches of many bunches and stored suspended in a cold, dry cellar or other room they will keep thru-out winter until spring, as I have seen in California. People store apples, as we did in Washington, so as to have them thru-out the year until summer comes again with strawberries, cherries and other fresh fruit. The Casaba and Honeydew melons are well adapted to be at their best in the springtime, stored just as one does squash.

As Apollo wrote in Hebrews 9:23, "The pattern of things which are heavenly should be purified by these," and in 11:3, "It is thru faith we understand that the worlds were framed by the Wisdom (Word) of God, so that the things which are seen came into being from those which are not seen." Thus John says in Apocalypse 4:3, "Round about the Throne was a Rainbow glistening like emeralds," and in 10:1, "And I saw another mighty angel coming down from heaven, clothed in a cloud; and the Rainbow of the cloud was upon his head, and his face was as the sun, and his legs as pillars of fire." These are the symbolic foreboding of the Essene Version of the reminder that the Elohim put in the Rainbow of Paradise as to God´s First Law of life in his Eternal covenant with Paradisian man. The Living Food cast down from Heaven thru the prism of the holy trinity in Spirit formed the twelve tints of the Rainbow to distill the Living Water of the Twelve Paradisian Fruits, one for each month, which are to cleanse man into becoming a vaporous essence allowing him to ascend heavenward like white light to the Throne of God midst paradise where such overcomers shall be given to eat of the Tree of Life. (Apoc.2:7) The ethereal gaseous elements, especially the H_2O of water vapor will lift up the Saints heavenward like a white cloud evaporating from a lake on a hot summer day, or in a whirl wind on a chariot with fiery white steeds, praising the glorious power of the Father. Alleluia! "Gather the clusters from the vineyards of earth for her grapes are fully ripe." And the winepress was trodden until the grape blood of Jesus shall save us all. (Apoc.14)

    Let us sing a new song before the Throne of God.

The Ascensional Science of Fruitarian Dietetics

AVOID A POISONED SOURCE OF CARPOPHAGOUS FOOD

After my 7 year month 7 day Spiritual Initiatory Period as a Son of God at the Temple of Metta-Aum (Lake Quilotoa), as well as before I went there to settle permanently for 4 years, I was taken to our present Propitiatory Shelter region for a "Camp of the Saints" in the Valley East of Quito. The Lord was testing me as to how full my Communion and Dedication to Him were. After leaving lake Quilotoa I had a choice of three things, either going to live in the snows of Mt. Chimborazo (which was an extreme ideal I was unprepared for), or returning to California to teach the world my Fruitarian Gospel, as well as remaining in Ecuador to live in the Valley east of Quito. But unwisely, since I was offered return fare to California, and I knew what delicious fruits were so easy to obtain there, I chose to go to live there a short time before returning to Ecuador for my home.

When I got to California, unlike back in 1938, by the beginning of 1950 the farmers fumigated all the fruits with the most deadly poisons that World War II science had discovered, Parathion to be specific, which was to harvest more deaths and crippling effects among farm workers than any other cause. Later, yet too late I found organic sources, but at the time no one suspected the consequences, and even with the knowledge of poisoned food people will choose poisoned food for economic reasons. This was the tremendous inadvertent obstacle that Spiritualizing Dietetics, Vitarianism ran up against and ruined the health of people attempting to live on juicy fruits. In the modern world of Maya, nothing can be trusted. The only sure way to have pure food is to grow it personally, provided you have uncontaminated soil and water resources. Land can be rented, leased or purchased if one is willing to work, since life on earth was given on the condition that man cares for the trees in his Garden of Paradise. Too many of us suppose that trees were to feed man and give him shade to lie and meditate under, and not that we propagate Paradise so others share in the benefits which we enjoy. Gradually the world is going organic, and less toxic poisons are being used, but in the meantime markets are still a poisoned source of food.

Even worse, the air of the cities is poisoned with smoke, carbon dioxide gas, industrial pollutants, and other contaminants. Growing ones own food out in the country-side where your breath of life is not poisoned starts producing the air you need to breathe from the chlorophyll of green plants or trees that provide you food. On these factors there are many books and periodicals available now, so let us go on to the information that is a military secret not publicly available.

GREEN PLANT CHLOROPHYLL CONCENTRATES RADIOACTIVE FALLOUT

Why is it that Dairy Products, Grains and Leafy Vegetables contain the greatest amount of Strontium 90 Radioactive Fallout? They are all the products of Chlorophyll concentrations in food. Wheat, grains and milk are not green, but nevertheless it is the chlorophyll that gives white milk of cows that eat grass, and even if the cows are fed unnaturally on grains. Grains are grass in origin and like leafy vegetables are rich in chlorophyll. Thus it singles out people in the U.S. as taking in the most Strontium 90 due to the American diet of dairy produce, wheat and leafy vegetables, if not beef which all come from chlorophyll concentrations. Ecuador gets the least fallout of all nations due to the unique sheltering by very high mountains cutting off the east-west descent of the fallout. The Roy Hoopes Report on Fallout in Food gave these figures: U.S. 15.4, Germany 13.6, United Kingdom 9.8, Vietnam 8.3, Japan 7.8, Peru 2.8, and Ecuador 1.2 on the daily intake of Strontium 90 micromicrocures. This is why Equatorial Andean Plateau identity is indisputable as to Propitiatory Shelter from nuclear fire raining from heaven as we interpret in our Handbook on Radioactive Fallout.

Now, our purpose in bringing out the chlorophyll Connection is to show the relation of an accumulating condemnation of all green herbage which in Genesis was given as the food of animals, while the Tree of Life as the Apocalypse confirms is the source of fruit and Living water.

Moreover, it is supported by scientific measurements showing the proportion of fallout being distributed by conditions in each country. The mountains have not moved and the distribution of rainfall, all are proportionate in the last half of the 20th century. Continuing the data given by Roy Hoopes as to Strontium 90 in food there is in Kale 74.7, Whole Wheat 56.2, String beans 43.2, Mustard Greens 40.0, Spinach 36.5, Turnip greens 32.0, Sweet potato 13.5, Cucumber 13.3 Turnip 10.6, Beets 10.3, Cabbage 7.1, Broccoli 5.3, Carrots 4.1, Radish 3.4, Celery 2.8, Cauliflower and Coconut 1.7, Potato 1.4, Lettuce 1.4, Peaches 1.1, Apples 1.0, Tomatoes 1.0. The reason fruits have the least is because their roots go deep into earth not contaminated, but the surface soil is concentrated with fallout as seen in wheat and dairy products, followed by kale and other leafy greens which have the most chlorophyll. Milk had the highest figures on Hoopes' lists.

There is another way to find how much chlorophyll, and thus the amount of magnesium is concentrating Strontium 90. It is in the chlorophyll of plants where magnesium is concentrated as we have

The Ascensional Science of Fruitarian Dietetics

been showing. Also the chemical affinity of elements, or mutual attraction, is determined by their position in the Periodic Table of Chemical Elements in which magnesium, calcium and strontium are in Group II and oxygen, sulfur and plutonium are in Group VI. This means all magnesium foods attract, or have affinity for Strontium 90 radioactive fallout, and all sulfur foods have an affinity for Plutonium 238 radioactive fallout which are of chief concern in long term health effects. As we show in our chart on amino acids, cystine and methionine have sulfur atoms in their molecules so as to have an affinity to Plutonium 238 fallout. Yet the reason for magnesium being of concern is because in Biological Transmutations Louis Kevran brought out that calcium in food is not assimilable, but magnesium is transmuted in calcium of our bodies.

    Thus we list the foods high in magnesium which have an affinity for Strontium 90 radioactive Fallout, as follows: Kelp 760, Wheat bran 490, Wheat germ 336. Almond 270, Cashew nut 267, Soybean 265, Brazil nut 206, Dulse 220, Peanut 206, Black walnut 190, Filbert 184, Sesame seed 181, Lima bean 180, Pea 180, wheat grain 160, pecan, beet greens 106, spinach 88, brown rice 88, lentil 80, Swiss chard 65, date 58, turnip greens 58, avocado 45, kale 37, kohlrabi 37, banana 33, and from there on the fruits continue as listed in our chart on page 21 of minerals, color and protein in fruits along with vegetables not yet mentioned. In the Roy Hoopes Report it shows wheat bran is 40% greater in Sr. 90 than whole wheat which tallies with the above magnesium content list along with sea weeds like kelp and Irish moss. The reason why Irish moss is fallout-heavy is because of the heavy rainfall in Irish Sea region and thus clouds sweeping into Wales give more fallout than in England and higher cancer death rate as we show in the Handbook on Radioactive Fallout. Also in our Growth Energy Food Chart tallies with our magnesium lists, with green leafy vegetables being high and the roots being next, altho as we explained the seeds are to be listed as potential Growth Energy foods, since they are banks of the growth energy ready to be sprouted into green plants. Growth Energy gives tumorous growth, and the chlorophyll-magnesium-affinity of the Sr. 90 fallout also gives tumorous growth in cancer and leukemia.

    "Altho there are foods containing more Sr. 90, so much milk is consumed by the average person that it is responsible for nearly half the total Sr. 90 ingested by the individual", writes Hoopes. Alfalfa has roots going deep in the earth like trees, but its surface roots cumulate more magnesium-chlorophyll and Growth Energy food, so that in Maryland

The Ascensional Science of Fruitarian Dietetics

the Sr. 90 was said to be 8 times the limit. It shows the strict fruitarian diet helps avoid Sr. 90.

In our Handbook on Radioactive Fallout we showed that Plutonium 238 threatens the destruction of great amount of inhabitants. Since 1998 was the year of the Holy Spirit, it provoked us to prophecy that 1999 will begin with more of cumulative disaster worldwide due to the weather, to be followed in the latter half by the return of the Cassini mission in the hope that the projectile will be able to gain velocity by a swing-by maneuver around the earth to propel it toward Saturn. This is only hoped for in action in which "the smallest misfire Cassini will be like a meteor, flaming into the earth´s atmosphere forcing the plutonium to disperse causing the most toxic chemical to get into people´s bodies," according to the N.Y. University nuclear physicists Dr. Michio Kaku.

This is predicted by numerous scientists to be a horrific day for humanity, causing Alan Cohen in a Anti-Cassini Demonstration out side Kennedy Space Center, as former NASA safety specialist, to declare the government had no right to take such a risk. As already explained plutonium has an affinity for sulfur, and the amino acids containing sulfur. One of these, Cystine, is necessary for red blood cells, tissue resistance to infection and the other, Methionine is a constituent of the hemoglobin, tissue and serum, vital to the function of the spleen, pancreas and lymph. These are found in apples, pineapple and other fruit beside the cabbage family.

The Apocalypse also predicted death, mourning and famine beside the raining of fire from the sky exactly as the scientists predict with Cassini projectile dispersing flamingly in the earth´s atmosphere like a meteor, all of which we detail in our Handbook on Radioactive Fallout and Camp of Saints booklet. Not only is fallout a horrific threat to the Chlorophyll eating people, but the Cassini projectile will contaminate those eating botanic fruits and ideal fruits grown outside of green houses, or not living in our equatorial Inter-Andean Propitiatory Shelter region of our Camp of Saints Project. However, the worst comes with protein, seeds, roots and green leaves that are both high in Magnesium and Sulfur. The latter half of the twentieth century was characterized by the intensity of diseases like leukemia, cancer, AIDS, etc. due to a half century of continuous daily, hourly and cumulative build-up of soil and food contamination of Strontium 90, and the guilty U.S. government is thus attempting suicide, with the Cassini projectile, rather than face the Nuremberg type trials for war crimes in its Space Wars maneuver, which has international protest and condemnation much worse than the suiciding Nazis.

In our schools we were taught that world War I was caused by the munitions makers, and war was a crime worse than others. But there is even greater reason why without nuclear poisoning of earth's inhabitants, the government is guilty of selling the people into bondage. The monetary system based on interest charged by the bankers had made them rich, while the public has been in slavery like in a monarchy and now no matter how much one earns, it will not provide the necessities of life. Inflation has spiralled upward to its limit, and thus the need to cover-up the greatest source of economic ruin without the scapegoat of blaming the troubles on communism, socialism, etc. This is why there is bound to be famine and widespread crime thru-out the cities since they are not producing food to feed population concentrations, and people will need to produce their own food or starve.

Human beings have a long history of error, all of which began when the devil impersonating Yahweh, a tribal god, cheated mankind from the Paradisian Way of Life. Not eating juicy fruits, going to nut and seed eating gave rise to passion, and the enzyme inhibitors prevented eating raw food, enslaving women to the cook stove and men to tilling earth for bread, cooked food and grazing cattle for animal products. Our earlier courses weaning people from cooking with the allowance of 20% cooked potatoes, etc. was an illusory compromise. It was followed by the allowance of lacto-bacterial products with the chlorophyll-rich greens, when all our efforts should have been in the direct path to Carpophagous nutrition without deluding compromises. Due to our own health in jeopardy, we return to the supreme importance of Living Water, the true Saviour of mankind in the strictly juicy fruit diet.

As to the complete protein necessity, with a variety of three fruits the Essential Amino Acids will be supplied. Pineapple has 11 of the Amino Acids, and Apples, Tomatoes and Cabbage have 10, so with a variety of the three, all of them will be supplied, or are able to give you still another showing that Growth Energy is distinct from Stability Energy, or staying power, of the Everlasting Life. The Calories or Energy Content of Seeds and Grains is Excessive, and the greens are deficient in extremes, the Carpophagous foods being the Middle Path.

The Ascensional Science of Fruitarian Dietetics

CALORIE ENERGY CONTENT FOR 100 GRAMS EDIBLE PORTION AND IF GROWTH ENERGY CHART LISTED (G.E.) or INDICATED AS VERSUS LASTING ENERGY

FOOD	G.E	FOOD	G.E
Seed and vegetable oil	884	Fresh figs	80
Pecan	687	Japanese persimmon	77
English Walnut	651	Parsnip	76
Brazil nut	654	Potato	76
Filbert	634	Prune type plum	75
Black Walnut	628	Jerusalem artichoke	75
Safflower seed	615	Black raspberry	73
Almond	598	Elderberry	72
Sesame seed	582	Carissa	70
Peanut	568	Sweet cherry	70
Cashew nut	661	American type grapes	69
Sunflower seed	560	European type grapes	69
Squash seed	553	Mango	66
Soybean	403	Damson plum	66
White rice	363	Strawberry guava	65
Wheat germ	363	Kumquat	65
Garbanzo	360	Soursop	65
Brown rice	360	Nectarine	64
Pinto bean	345	Pomegranate	63
Lima bean	345	Blackberry	62
Dehydrated prune	344	Guava	62
Red bean	343	Loganberry	62
Dehydrated banana	340	Sour red cherry	58
White bean	340	Red raspberry	57
Lentil	340	Apple	56
Mung bean	340	Roseapple	56
Broad bean	338	Black currant	54

The Ascensional Science of Fruitarian Dietetics

CALORIE ENERGY CONTENT FOR 100 GRAMS EDIBLE PORTION AND IF GROWTH ENERGY CHART LISTED (G.E.) or INDICATED AS VERSUS LASTING ENERGY

FOOD	G.E	FOOD	G.E
Rye	334	Groundcherry	53
Sorghum grain	332	Pineapple	52
Wheat	330	Apricot	51
Red Hot Pepper	321	Pitanga	51
Raisin	289	Red/white currant	50
Rice bran	276	Winter squash	50
Dried apple	275	Orange	49
Date	274	Loquat	48
Fig dried	274	Japanese plum	48
Dried peach	268	Globe Artichoke	47
Dried apricot	260	Cranberry	46
Dried prune	255	Tangerine	46
Tamarind	239	Brussels sprouts	45
Olive Mission	184	Dandelion greens	45
California avocado	128	Parsley	44
Garlic	137	Beet	43
Olive Ascolano	129	Pricklypear	42

The Ascensional Science of Fruitarian Dietetics

FOOD	G.E	FOOD	G.E
Florida avocado	128	Carrot	42
Persimmon	127	Grapefruit	41
Sapote	125	Celeriac	40
Plantain	119	Collard	40
Sweet potato	114	Gooseberry	39
Jujube	105	Papaya	39
Breadfruit	103	Peach	39
Custard apple	101	Kale	38
Yam	101	Onion	38
Jackfruit	98	Strawberry	37
Taro	78	Carambola	35
Sweet corn	96	Mung bean sprouts	35
Cherimoya	94	Honeydew melon	33
Sugarapple	94	Broccoli	32
Olive Sevillano	93	Red cabbage	31
Red banana	90	Mustard greens	31
Granadilla	90	Sweet red pepper	31
Sapodilla	89	Canteloupe	30
Common banana	85	Turnip	30

The Ascensional Science of Fruitarian Dietetics

FOOD	G.E	FOOD	G.E
Pawpaw	85	Kohlrabi	29
Lemon	27	Lime	28
Casaba melon	27	Cauliflower	27
Watermelon	26	Asparagus	26
Pumpkin	26	Spinach	26
Eggplant	25	Swiss chard	25
Beet greens	24	Cabbage	24
Tomato	22	Coconut water	22
Endive	20	N.Z. Spinach	19
Summer squash	19	Watercress	19
Lettuce	18	Towelgourd	18
Celery	17	Radish	17
Rhubarb	16	Cucumber	15

JUICES

Orange	45		
Tangerine	43	Grapefruit	39
Apple	47	Lemon	25
Lime	26		

The Ascensional Science of Fruitarian Dietetics

The Fruit diet has very little bibliographical precedents, but we shall quote D.L.M. Abramowski, M.D., Ch.D., M.D.H., Senior Physician to the District Hospital, Mildurea, Australia. "Up to my 50th year I lived on the common mixed diet. I had meat, bread, vegetables, a little fruit, etc. all cooked; I drank tea, coffee, beer and whiskey, and smoked cigars. I grew stout and heavy, and, altho I did my work as a physician and surgeon with the usual amount of success, I began to feel I would not be able to stand the strain of active life much longer,...Palpitations of the heart, sleeplessness, headaches, rheumatic and digestive troubles and other disorders made their appearance. An examination of my arteries proved them to be in a progressive state of hardness and brittleness, arterio-sclerosis. The miracle has happened! My arteries have carried safely, thru 10 more active and strenuous years and they are in a much better condition to-day than they were 20 years ago." Thus, he describes his rejuvenation on fruit. Then he describes his success in treating patients with fruit and fruit juices, without any drugs or unnatural alimentation in typhoid, appendicitis and other diseases, and his nurses since 1903 became fruitarians themselves and got stronger and healthier than before.

This we learn from his treatise, "Fruitarian Diet and Physical Rejuvenation". He also quotes Dr. Josiah Oldfield, the well known London surgeon and superintendent of the fruitarian "Lady Margaret" Hospital at Bromley, England, "which proves the immense benefit of the regimen similar to our own in surgical cases". Dr. Oldfield was the founder of the Fruitarian Society, and stated he had experience, or "done over 2,000 operations on patients treated on the fruitarian dietary, and have come to the conclusion that to obtain the best results it is well to put the patient on a fruitarian dietary a month before operation. I have lost only one case after operation during the last ten years." Then Dr. Abramowski reveals what his concept of a fruit-eater consists of: "Man evolved on food consisting of fruits, especially palm fruits, grains, and nuts. His teeth and digestive organs are most perfectly adapted for this diet, even more than those of his immediate forerunners,- the man-like apes. Man was forced to his unnatural food by terrestrial catastrophes... Cooking not only changes the albumen by coagulating it, but it also detaches from the albumen-molecule the food salt; it tears these out of their organic combination and reduces them into lifeless inorganic matter.. The soft, luscious thirst and hunger-quenching fruits and the solid, heat-and-strength-giving and body-building nuts and grains."

The Ascensional Science of Fruitarian Dietetics

As we have shown in "Vitalogical Hygiene", the theory of Evolution of Darwinism was a farce, since the apes devolved from man, and took on characteristics of huge herbivore, since the gorilla, chimpanzee, orangutan, etc. live on generally 50% jungle greens and 50% true fruits. When the large apes began using coconuts from palms, they devolved into small monkeys, and they into squirrels using walnuts, acorns etc. and the greater use of seeds and grains developed keratinous tissue going from flying squirrels, lemurs, etc. came the flying fowls or birds. As to digestive organs, man was without a gizzard to grind the seed-grains since teeth in humans are absolutely inadequate.

In our book "Those Strong, Powerful and Extraordinary Vegetarians" we told of pomiculturist fruitarians who in a case of a Persian has not eaten other things but fresh-fruit uncooked since youth, rarely taking a little wholegrain rye bread. This system was taught by German naturalist Gustavo Schlickeysen, author of "Fruit and Bread" which establishes man as frugivorous. Well, it is an established fact that man was not given baking ovens in Paradise, and the cooking destroys the food value of bread, and eating grains raw, as well as nuts or other seeds they are inhibited from being digested, requiring the wasting of the vitality, altho stimulating our passion, just as cooking destroys the plant enzymes. So the theories of scientists based on Evolution and Nutritionists based on seed and chlorophyll proteins are false assumptions, since they allow only two and a half centuries at the most, but the Bible Patriarch's thousand year nearness and certain thousand year old Jains of Mt. Abu India who live on figs, show that man was originally Everlasting in the fullness of Godhood. The present advocates of strictly juicy fruits exclusively turn out to be users of nuts.

After the "Bread and Fruit" promotion of grains in early 20th century the latter 20th century took to more in demand for sprouted grains and wheat grass as a supposed remedy, giving superior leaf protein and chlorophyll to solve problem of the lack of red blood corpuscles, lack of blood clotting and calcium deficiencies coming from poisoning of all food with pesticides, herbicides and soil mineral exhaustion which was the reason for giving up grains and leaf food in fruitarianism. Yet hidden from public information as a military secret was the direct and preponderant factor in red cell deficiency. The erythrocyte (red) cells are formed by the erythroblast nucleated cells in the bone marrow but now a disruption with Strontium 90 fallout in bone matter gave man bone cancer. Strontium 90 causes bone cancer and leukemia in bone marrow but begins with anemia. <u>The terrifying</u>

<u>increase of Strontium 90 levels in the human bones, milk, wheat and leafy greens was so negative causing people to refuse such foods</u> in first decade of the Nuclear Era, that the U.S. military arms race was almost disrupted, <u>making for the information ban.</u> By then it was 70 units, but over 4 decades Strontium 90 has been coming down from blasts of nuclear weapons heavily contaminating the soil, food and man. Thus, what makes people sensitive to food poisons is the basic cause in bone marrow formation of erythrocytes. Likewise, it weakens resistance to air pollution and most all disease. "Just one automobile moving along Los Angeles freeways needs as much air to disperse its waste products as do the people in the county for breathing". (Dr. P.A. Leighton)

Your editor witnessed a dramatic effect after living in Quito and Otavalo from 1958 to 1962, but then spending 35 years in fallout region of Loja and Cuenca he had a resumption of near-death effects from Parathion and other agro-poisons that gave him paralysis due to California fruit industry employment. Then returning to the Quito region protected shelter from the high equatorial Andes, after one year (1998) in 7 year renewal of all the body cells, he no longer was affected seriously due to agro-poisons combined with Strontium 90 similar to living there in 1958-1962 as a fruitarian. In that contaminated region likewise the author had to give up his fruitarian ideals, like elsewhere in especially the northern temperate zone. As Roy Hoopes reported children who need more bone calcium took in heavy amounts of Strontium 90.

The Ascensional Science of Fruitarian Dietetics

COSMIC LEVITATIONAL FORCES

"The sugar produced from starch when hydrogen acts upon it has a tendency to go further in the same direction, toward etherealization. Flower scents, known to chemists as etheric oils, all contain a great deal of hydrogen.... Cosmic Levitational Forces, dominant in the upper part of plants, work upon starch of middle zone and etherealize it into sugar." (The Nature of Substance, by Dr. Rudolf Hauschka) Dr. Hauschka uses the term Levitational Force for what we have called sublimal and Ascensional forces or energies, in contrast to our avoidance of Growth Energy, reproductive forces or earthy gravitational powers. Also Hauschka agrees that: "A survey of changing levels of consciousness in human evolution shows how they are reflected in changes in man's food." Biological Transmutations upheld by Kevran, was preceded by Hauschka saying, "Not only that plants can transform substances, but that the creation of basic elements of matter is commonplace in the organic kingdoms. Herzeele's experiments offer tangible proof that the supposed immutability of chemical elements is a fiction that must be speedily discarded if natural science is to progress." However, one must study the works of these Paradisian New Age pioneers to get into the basics of Levitational studies.

Your author's numerous experiences in physical levitation and bilocation witnessed by friends can readily be attributed to the fruit sugar of his juicy fruit diet and his life at super-altitudes in the High Andes, as testified in "MAITREYA, THE LOVEWISDOM AUTOBIOGRAPHY". Moreover, the etherealization and biological transmutation of elements described by Heerzle, Hauschka and Kevran can only be accounted for by a gravitational and levitational classification of elements of the periodical table of chemical elements. Reincarnation, Karma and Nirvana beside Ascension are proven by living witnesses of how individuals, or ethereal spiritual entities are earth-bound thru numerous lives unable to overcome the earth's gravitational binding power (called Karma in the East) and not just "hell fire" of Christian religious beliefs, and likewise the final liberation in Nirvana or the Ascension.

"Does it not seem high time to counter the dogma of matter's preexistence with the preexistence of Spirit?" writes Haushka showing the definite connection between earthly substance and planetary happenings. He thus published graphs to show the moon rhythm was subservient to a stronger annual, or the sun's rhythm. The so-called Age

The Ascensional Science of Fruitarian Dietetics

of Enlightenment reduced man to a mere creature of necessity ruled by animal necessity. "The eternal creative music of the universe became the monotonous rattling of a giant mill driven by the stream of chance and floating on it,- a mill sufficient unto itself without a maker or miller, a real perpetuum mobile, with only itself to grind." This Hauschka relates to stating: "The human body described by anatomy is only the physical aspect of man´s eternal being, so Goethe´s view, was light a far more loftier element than the sphere in which its waves were manifest. He spoke of light´s moral qualities, of deeds and sufferings as the origin of color... Light waves were merely the manifestation of eternal indivisible light." Thus, our study of the sun´s effect on "Growth Energy" are substantiated by the opponents of materialistic science in philosophy and higher biological science which we call "Vitalogical Sciences".

This introduction is followed by the study of the chemical elements of substance. At a 100 miles up in the stratosphere, hydrogen shows a concentration of 99.5% illustrating why zeppelins rise up. This is the reason why the author was clairvoyantly drawn, not only to the equatorial Andes, but to the "Land closest to the sun" rather than the tropical lowlands. In the lowland the barometric pressure shows the heaviest concentration of carbon dioxide, methane, etc. due to the decomposition of green jungle vegetation. <u>Carbon dioxide is the heaviest gas</u> which in the "Dog´s Grotto" covers the earth's surface where dogs die from suffocation. So rather than the low dense carbon dioxide predominant air our fruitarians should seek at least the oxygen-rich air above the subtropical altitudes, and then try to adapt to the "prana" and <u>hydrogen rich super-altitudes</u> of Tibetan and Himalayan Masters or now the <u>High Andes</u> in the New Age. This is why Mdme. H.P. Blavatsky, master K.H. Pr. O.M. Chenrezi Lind and other authorities claimed the World´s Spiritual Center in the Paradisian Golden Age now is in the Equatorial Andes, the "New Tibet" and Himalayas, just as did the Bible Apocalypse and Eastern Scriptural prophecy. Likewise, not only do the spiritual entities reincarnate, being born and dying in countless lifetimes, but the matter they are embodied with continually is materializing and dematerializing, as we remember from physical levitational and bilocational experiences.

Dr. Rudolf Hauschka also supports the equatorial super-altitudinal idea with his New Age biochemist transmutational arguments. "Therefore <u>cosmic rhythms are mirrored only in the middle region</u> of both man and earth. This leads to a harmonizing rhythm of earth and

The Ascensional Science of Fruitarian Dietetics

sun (as cosmic representative). Where earth forces gain the upper hand, as at the poles, or where life is dominated by cosmic radiating forces, as at the equator... High summer is the season of oxygen's polar opposite, hydrogen; a subtle fire process which everywhere dissolves form and etherealizes matter." As already described Hauschka speaks of cosmic levitational forces dominating in sugar and acid-containing fruits of summertime as now in equatorial super-altitudes. So the solar plexus of man, as well as earth's "land closest to the sun", both predominate with rarified hydrogen or "prana" concentrations and sun-ripened fruits.

In a triangle intuitive chart illustrated in the Lovewisdom Auto-biography, the high summer constellation of Leo the Lion shows Ecuador as the author's place for initiation as the Son of the Sun of the sun, meaning Son of God, which Hauschka describes as symbolized by the Lion "with flaring mane surrounded the head like a golden aura, of flaming courage and firey attitude of soul". To this he adds, "Leo, the Lion, is in this sense the representative of fire-related forces radiating from his segment of the universe into all levels of activity and manifestation: the soul-spiritual, the biological, the mineral. Their final manifestation is hydrogen and its activity; here the sublime process comes to rest. One cannot help thinking of the adage, Matter is the last step on the path to God." This may corroborate reasons why the writer was chosen as the Spiritual Father for the New Race and Age. Hydrogen is common to all acids chemically known also to be found in most juicy fruits, along with fruit sugar and living water.

Our Sublimal and Growth Energy Chart given at the beginning of this book, shows that the ideal fruits with sugar and acid combined with living water as yielding the sublimal energy, along with the botanic fruits as well as the acidophilus bacteria-forming blossoms such as cabbage, cauliflower, broccoli, which predominate with ascensional forces of hydrogen pre-dominant in upper parts of plants which etherealize starches into sugars.

This quality of acids in fruits enables them even to dissolve metallic poisons deposited in the body, as well as the calcareous accumulations from eating grains, drinking inorganic earth-water, to replace them with living water organic elements. Herein people were deceived in thinking that fasting on inorganic earth water, or adding man-made bread or wheat grass or sprouts, purified fruitarians. "Now the question arises whether this tendency is to be regarded as a purely physical

The Ascensional Science of Fruitarian Dietetics

phenomenon of anti-gravity, or as the last visible remnant of a cosmic fire-force that pervades the universe as a dissolving, de-materializing element?" writes Hauschka. It was living on tree-ripened oranges and grapefruit in Florida that enabled my witnessing with a friend actual descending from the air in <u>physical levitation</u> from the dematerialized ethereal entity and returning to the solid physical form. The materializing force of Growth Energy in green leafage, as in springtime, and in the sublimating warmth of summer brings forth the ethereal marvel of the blossom, pouring itself out into the universe as fragrance, color, pollen-dust. This idea Hauschka illustrates: "Investigations of the stratosphere are credited with discovering clouds of pollen, still mounting skyward, many miles above earth."

    He then follows telling of flower scents containing a great deal of hydrogen, volatile wanting to fly away and highly inflammable like the etheric oils of orange peels, evergreen tree twigs, etc. His beauteous description is added, "The physiological processes accompanying the spiritual fire called enthusiasm are hydrogen-based. A fire-force works in our enthusiasm which, radiating from the heart, warms our entire being. It actually makes us feel as tho our blood were lighter." Herein I have described the effects of Nirvakalpa Samadhi, the Ecstacy of the intimate Presence of God within, that keeps one full of grace even in times of trial as well as everyday efforts in God-ward ascension.

    Our book review report on Hauschka's "Nature of Substance" should suffice with the mention of <u>oxygen</u>, since "it <u>accounts</u> for almost <u>90% of water</u>," so that our <u>emphasis</u> of Biblical <u>"Living Water" of Everlasting Life</u> gains scientific importance. He in turn prefers to call oxygen "biogen" or "life-substance", just as he prefers "pyrogen" or fire-substance for hydrogen. Hauschka adds: "Life oscillates between form and fire, rigidity and dissolution." To illustrate this he presents graphs of the characteristic rhythm of even alternations, with full moon favoring the emergence of substance and new moon favoring its disappearance as shown in seedlings. "But, the moon is both an earth satellite and reflector of the entire cosmos, particularly the sun and its movement thru the Zodiac."

    We have mentioned our publisher in India, Dr. J.D. Narula, being celebrated as the nation's longest living person at the time, and that he used fruits and green peas as a staple in this diet, but it should not be construed into that immature seeds are an ideal food for the average person, and especially younger men and women, since they are particularly Passion-Producing. When one reaches the average longevity of 70 years, from there on up beyond a century, people do not have sexual losses. We have also mentioned the two centuries old pomiculturist who lived on fruit and rarely ate a little bread. Your author also experienced effects as a brain food in parsley. But here we are in a Growth Energy factor that gives semen its embryonic tumor producing factor due to its high phosphorus content, 63 mg., similar to the green peas with 116 mg. So the greatest acid-forming element, Phosphorus, is in the class with the semen and passion-producing foods. Your editors error in "Vitalogical Hygiene" particularly was to use curds, or fresh cheese, with casein rich in phosphorus, which is even higher in goat's milk, as well as eggs. Cholesterol was first isolated from gall stones, which result from pasteurized milk products. Cholesterol is abundant in the brain, nerves, semen and ova, beside tumors. So these cause albuminuria and nephritis. Fasting increases the purine end products, it is notable in the incubation of eggs which is a growth energy phenomenon, and especially noted in those eating liver and other glands. Bodansky shows the ratio of Calcium to Phosphorus to be 1:5.7 in oatmeal, 1:14.8 in wheatgerm, 1:16 in Rye flour, 1:10.7 in Rice, and 1:9 in barley, which is believed to be the significant anti-calcifying factor in cereals. Thus, it is the albuminoids in keratin proteins found in grass and milk of herbivorous animals and grains and other seeds of granivorous birds which are high in phosphorus that cause the various acid-forming results.

As to <u>Anti-Enzyme inhibiting digestion</u> we found that Bodansky's Physiological chemistry of <u>1927</u> already describing it (long before Dr. Howell), noted that <u>radioactivity was attributed to inhibiting</u> the <u>changing of starch into sugars</u>, which Hauschka attributes to be a <u>levitational force</u>. This we believe is the adverse factor in this aspect as to our fruitarian students living in Spain eating ideal fruits but using wheat grass juice for Chlorophyll, which give results in high radioactive fallout concentration, similar to grass products like milk and salad greens. Another anti-enzyme factor inhibiting metabolism and levitational forces are obviously the salts of heavy metals such as mercury, silver, lead, arsenic and copper. This gives reason for the removing of 32 mercury-silver fillings in the author's teeth in 1940 before leaving Florida to come to Ecuador. Antiseptics inhibit Lipase, and chlorine in tap water used to wash foods inhibit amylase, maltose, ptylain, rennin and urease. Likewise Fluorides have a pronounced effect on lipase metabolism. Autolysis, or self-digestion is also inhibited by asphyxia in low barometric pressure such as your author experienced in the lower equatorial tropics. The flow of gastric juice is inhibited by spicy condiments, alcohol, anger, fear and fever. The flow of gastric juice prevents intestinal putrefication and hot humid lowlands prevent the oxidation of carbohydrates so as to give nausea when eating or even the smell of bananas and sweet fruits. In turn the gastric hunger contraction may be inhibited by hyperglycemia, the excess of blood sugar alternated with its lack.

In connection with the Vilcabamba centenarians, with whom fruit played a prominent part in their diet along with animal fats first from fresh cheese but in modern time raw pig fat, the chief factor could have been the lack of Phosphorus in the soil and cooked yucca in their diet. However, this is definitely the factor in Saint John's Bread, Carob, being only with 1 mg. phosphorus, altho the other fruits he ate may have a little more. This harmonizes with his doctrine of Everlasting Life, in sublimal, levitational forces. Along with Dr. Alexis Carrel's affirmation of man being the heir to immortal life, inhibited due to "Biological sin," another Nobel laureate, Linus Pauling said,- "Death is unnatural...man is theoretically immortal." Other scientists attribute disease and death to progressive acid saturation.

However, Heerzle, Hauschka and Kevran found calcium does not transmute from plants to bones and teeth, but rather calcium is changed into phosphorus in humans and animals. Nature turns the most alkaline element into the most characteristically acid-forming one. It is magnesium in foods that gives us calcium in bones, teeth and body. Thus, phosphorus was erroneously believed to be a brain food, but disappears transformed into sulfur, another acid forming element appearing in amino acids with heavy molecular weight, or anti-levitational. Noting these details we give a list of PHOSPHORUS HIGH FOODS, which were not included in the List of Fruits relating Color to Protein and Minerals on Page 21. Rice bran 1386, Wheat bran 1276, Pumpkin and Squash seed 1144, Rice polishings 1102, Sunflower seed 837, Brazil nuts 693, Sesame seed 616, Black walnut 570, Soybean 554, Almond 504, cowpea 426, White bean 425, Peanut 401, Red bean 406, Peanut with skin 401, Wheat 394, Broadbean 391, Lima bean 385, Durum wheat 386, English walnut 380, Lentil 377, Rye 376, Cashew nut 373, Hickory nut 360, Mung bean 340, Pea 340, Gilbert 337, Chickpea 331, Millet 311, Pearled barley 290, Dulse 267, Hot red pepper 240, Kelp 240, Soybean fresh 225, Brown rice 221, Garlic 202, Coconut 187, Irish moss 157, Lima bean fresh 142, Dried peach 117, Green peas 116, Celeriac 115, Tamarind 113, Sweet corn 111, Kale leaves 93,

The Ascensional Science of Fruitarian Dietetics

Collard leaf 82, Brussels sprouts 80, Dried Prune 79, Jerusalem artichoke 78, Dried figs 77, Parsnip 77, Yam 69, Soybean sprouts 67, Dandelion greens, Mung bean sprouts 64, Parsley 63, Asparagus 62, Turnip greens 58, Endive 54, Watercress 54, Potato 53, Dried apple 52, Leek 50, Mustard greens 50, Pear dried 48, New Zealand spinach 46, Beet greens 40, Swiss chard 39, Carrot 36, Onion 36, Radish 31, Turnip 30, Celery 28, Iceberg lettuce 22.

    Finally, we come to how much fruit can a man use for health living an ever-lasting life? Remember Tolstoy's tale of how much land can a man use, in which free land was parcelled out in amounts a man could travel marking out in one day, so a man circumscribed all he could but at nightfall he died of exhaustion to get back before dark. So one must be very prudent in amounts eaten, easily overdone on juicy fruit which people judge as least harmful, or "more the better". In the CALORIE-ENERGY CHART it shows 100 gram edible portions, - see page 27. But that is one tenth kilogram, a kilogram being 1,000 grams or is recommended 2100 calories full grown. There are 3 large apples per lb., 12 apricots, 3 bananas, 12 figs, 4 peaches. Measured in grams, 1 apple 150 g., 3 apricots 114 g., 1/2 avocado 108 g., 1 banana 150 g. 1 cup blackberries 144 g., 1/2 cantaloupe 385 g., 1 cup cherries 130 g., 1 cup dates 178 g. 3 figs 114 g., 1/2 grapefruit 285 g., 1 cup grapes 160 g., 1 Navel orange 180 g., papaya 1 cup 182 g., 1 peach 114 g., 1 pear 182 g., 1 persimmon 125 g., 1 cup pineapple 140 g., 1 cup raspberries 123 g., 1 cup strawberries 149 g., 1 tangerine 114 g., 1 tomato 150 g., 1 cup cabbage 100 g., cauliflower 1 cup 120 g.

    One fruit should be eaten in one meal to avoid gas and digestive inhibition, and at least 6 hours later another type of fruit may be eaten, preferably acid or sub-acid fruit in 10 o'clock meal and sweet fruit in afternoon meal at 4, before fasting until 10 AM again, with Saturday or Sunday a complete fast over 24 hours as your day of rest.

HEAVENLY ECCLESIA THEOLOGY
OF ESSENE BASIS IN BRIEF

    Scientists studying the genealogy of the breeding and culture of fruit trees have shown Paradisians have lived a 100 million years on earth eating fruit exclusively. Even 12 million years ago man's teeth were not eroded by other course food. Herodotus confirmed Greek traditions about the Hyperboreans living at the polar regions with an eternal springtime climate eating tree fruits exclusively. With a change in the axis of the earth, the poles froze, just as we show will come about due to ecological crisis disaster immediately in the third millennium beginning THE RETURN OF THE PARADISIAN NEW AGE, as told in our "Mystical Anthropology" and is the Lovewisdom Message for our founding of our mystical order of "Paradisians"

Now the Buddhists tell of their Tathagatha teachers existing tens and hundreds of thousands of years ago. After them when Buddhist Missionaries appeared as "Gymnosophists" (Naked Sages) in Egypt and Palestine, the West labelled them as "Essenes" or Pythagorians. The fact was documented in the elder Pliny's "Natural History":

"The Essenes had established themselves in the west at the Dead Sea, far enough from (the city) to avoid its obnoxious effects. They lead a solitary life different from that of all other men. They have no wives, having forsaken the love of women. The date palm trees are their only partners. Their ranks are swelled by the arrival of new converts, the large number of whom are drawn there due to their distaste for ordinary life or because of some rebuff in fortune. Thus, unbelievable as it may appear, there has existed for hundreds of thousands of years an everlasting government in which no children have been born, but whose expansion is the result of penitence." This is why John came preaching "Do Penance for the Government of God is with us!" The Essenes had come west from Buddhist origins, so at 13 John went to study in a Buddhist Monastery in Nepal for 6 years.

We progressed in history only to illustrate these aspects, but Essene Scriptures, the Book of Adam and Eve, tell of figs the size of watermelons due to uneroded fertility of earth and Seth and his children dwelt at the foot of their Paradisian Garden eating exclusively of the juicy nectarous fruits on Mt. Hermon, the home of the apricot, beside its peaches, figs and other delicious fruits all existing on that holy mountain.

This Essene lore continues in the Dead Sea Scroll version of the Old Testament, on to Philo of Alexandria (20 B.C. 40 A.D.) Who describes the sects devoted to the Contemplative Life, Pythagoreans and other Greeks, the Magi, the Buddhist Gymnosophists and the Essenes who number 4,000. All of these abstain from animal sacrifices and married life, diametrically against orthodox Jewish doctrines. Philo elaborates on their shunning life in the cites, holding wealth in common and never making weapons, or anything useful in war, and hold to strict moral precepts, fulfilling the laws of prehistoric ancestry (Buddhist origin in East Asia). In turn, Josephus (37-110 A.D.) already tells of new mitigation of principles allowing cooked food, marriage and bearing children, contrary to the pristine purity of their Paradisian perfection as seen in Pliny's description of the Dead Sea community.

The Ascensional Science of Fruitarian Dietetics

As we related in the "Buddhist Essene Gospel of Jesus" the Old Testament tells of two Messiahs, as does the "Manual of Discipline" of the latter Dead Sea Covenanters, Essenes carrying arms, and teach battle strategy. John's Gospel is directed opposing these backsliders, and his assembly of Apostles at Bethany on the Jordan was thus favored by Herod Antipas who esteemed his guidance in politics against the Zealots and their political King of the Jews, Simon of Galilee who was crucified as the Zealot Messiah by Pilate's soldiers. Meanwhile, at the pseudo-Essene colony of latter Dead Sea Qumran, the Teacher of Righteousness laments their wayward backsliding: "God has given it to his Chosen as an everlasting possession, He has made them co-inheritors of the saints, he has brought them into closest union with the sons of Heaven, To form an Assembly, one sacred foundation eternally established for all time. (Obviously John's) As for me, I am evil, my crimes, my sins, my backsliding, has set me among the wicked carnal multitudes. The perversity of my heart makes me as vermin and those who walk in darkness. Righteousness is with God and from his hand comes perfect living! By his knowledge all things exist." (Manual of Discipline, -referring to John's Essenes)

In turn, the "Psalms of Solomon" envision a king rather than priest "Their King is the Anointed Lord... All powerful thru his hope in God, Subdue the earth by his Word for ever. He will bless the people of the Lord in Wisdom with gladness, he will be pure of sin, rule over countless and destroy sinners by the might of his Word... For God has made him strong by his Holy Spirit." We note the very words of John in all these Essene Scriptures. Likewise in the Testament of Levi we cite: "After their punishment their priesthood shall fail, then shall the Lord raise up a new priest... With the Father's Voice. In his priesthood the Gentiles shall be multiplied in the knowledge of the Lord. And he shall open the gates of Paradise, And shall remove the threatening sword against Adam. And he shall give to the saints to eat from the Tree of Life, and the Holy Spirit shall be upon them and the Saints shall be clothed with joy."

Thus, these Essene prophets before John lauded the Holy Anointing Spirit of the word in the Presence of the Apostle Beloved of Christ. Levi like John emphasized that the fruitarian diet enables the Camp of the Saints to be Anointed by the Holy Spirit, just as John's Gospel tells of the mighty works enabled by the Presence of Jesus' Anointing Spirit. However, Apollo, learned in Essene doctrines of Philo's Alexandrian Essenes, joins John as a dissenter of the latter

The Ascensional Science of Fruitarian Dietetics

pseudo-Essene backsliders who are bread eaters and wife-bonded often, and in the Epistle to these Hebrews preaches about <u>the New Priesthood</u> in the <u>Order of Melchizedek,</u> and his <u>grape blood</u> Communion with the Father´s Spirit of Grace in His Son. Apollo calls the Old Covenant obsolete, coming to perfect the New Testament which has High Priest seated at the right hand of the Throne of Majesty in Heaven, who put his Law into our minds and writes it in our hearts. This Melchizedek was the king of Salem (Peace) whose name means King of righteousness, and his <u>priesthood abides forever,</u> without birth or death. We must ascend to heaven, to the Throne of Grace, earned both by faith and works. Apollos, as the Apostle of John, causes Paul to be driven out of Greece as John´s Assemblies drove him out of Phrygia. Among the dissenters against Paul in Thessalonia, is Silvanus who with Mark travel to Babylon to join Peter, and thus Silvanus proceeds for Babylon for missionary work in Egypt preaching Apollo and John´s teaching to sectarian Essenes that Philo describes. Thus we come to the earliest Christian Hermit, Paul, replacing the anti-Christian backsliding teaching of Paul, wine bibber and eater of sacrificed animals. Paul the Hermit dwells in a cavern eating and clothing himself like John on the Jordan with date palm fiber. John´s date palm fiber loin cloth, is not camel´s hair but in Aramaic means rope fiber. This was true to the Essene Dead Sea original colony that the elder Pliny describes. Paul the Hermit after 90 years solitary life is found by Anthony, from whom Christian solitary life is credited as the founder of monasticism and Religious contemplatives. Now various hermits lived on 15 figs a day, just as John´s food included figs at Cana, where Nathanael, his Apostle was his host. The 15 fresh figs a day regimen is the necessary frugality needed to acquire the Anointing of the Holy Spirit, rather than becoming "full of new wine and speaking in diverse tongues", (Acts 2:13) showing how fruitarians will delude themselves <u>eating excessively of fruit</u> and be <u>disappointed</u> when they do not develop clairvoyant vision or <u>Divine Rapture.</u>

    These facts we bring out as to John´s true fruitarian followers, and all of them base this True theology on the Pristine Perfection of the Paradisian Essenes. "In the Beginning" on earth for man, "GOD SAID: BEHOLD I MAKE EVERY PLANT AND EVERY TREE WHICH YIELDS SEED FOR PROPAGATING ITS OWN SPECIES: THEIR <u>FRUIT IS FOR MAN´S FOOD</u>, AND THE GREEN HERBAGE IS FOR THE LIVING SENTIENT BEINGS THAT FLY AND MOVE UPON THE EARTH." (Modern Clarified Version) this was God´s First

The Ascensional Science of Fruitarian Dietetics

Law of Life for Mankind and their diet. Then, in the second chapter of Genesis, it elaborates exactly on this <u>eternal law</u>: "And Yahweh Elohim brought forth all manner of trees, fair to behold and pleasant to eat of: The Tree of Life also in the midst of Paradise, and the Tree of Knowledge of Good and Evil... And commanded them saying: Of every Tree of Paradise thou shall eat, but of the tree of the Knowledge of Good and Evil thou shall not eat. For in the day so ever thou shall eat of it thou shall be dying unto death." Thus the various Hebrew, Aramaic, Greek, Catholic, Protestant Versions, are clarified by our modern version, because as they interpreted it, it appeared as if man was told to eat seeds, nuts, grains or herbage, all of which are disease and death productive as we have illustrated. Thus, the Tree of the Knowledge of Good and Evil is present in seeds, nuts, grains, legumes, roots and green leafage. John directed his Unveiling of Jesus Christ to the Seven Ecclesia of the Essene, showing that each of the Seven Assemblies were democratically autonomous. Yet his first assembly was at Bethany on the Jordan, followed by that at Cana, and later he was in Jerusalem, so in no way can such assemblies be called churches, as the roman church avers. They all are Christian, yet each hold to their inspired interpretation of what religion is. Mark, the son of Simon Peter the fisher, affirms immediately after the election of the twelve apostles, that Jesus said: "If a kingdom is divided against itself, that kingdom cannot stand. And if Satan rises up against himself and is divided, he cannot stand, but that is his end." Thus, Peter the fisherman's son, Mark, prophetically described the fall of the Roman Religion, and the Reign of the Papal Monarchy in Religion. Likewise, John's Apocalypse prophecies that the city built on seven mountains, was Babylon the Great, while the supposed first Pope, wrote his First Epistle from Babylon. As to the official Roman Church Theologian, Thomas Aquinas, who refers to Paul as "The Apostle", as if Paul was sent to found the Church in Rome supposedly with Peter, who never set foot in Rome, this is plainly a household divided against itself. <u>Paul divided himself against the Three Pillars of Jerusalem's original Congregation, James, Peter and John,</u> justifying himself by faith against the works of the flesh, (Gal. 2:9-22) In turn John declares that Paul is led by the Spirit of the Anti-Christ (I-Jn.4:3) which is the "spirit of error", because he violates God's commandments and freely goes to eat flesh from the butcher's shop (I.Cor.10:25-27) or whatever is set on the table, being completely against the Essene principles of abstinence from animal flesh, obtained by bloodshed or otherwise, clearly condemning his teaching at the Council of Apostles and bishops in Jerusalem, (Acts 15:20) beside teaching marriage, rather than be begotten by God, and those who waste their seed are "Children of the devil" (I-Jn..3:9) and the Gospel of Matthew says one must become an eunuch for the Kingdom of Heaven.

However, John's Gospel begins at Bethany, or Simon's Banana Plantation, after he gathers two disciples, James and Andrew, who with Simon, convert Philip and Nathanael. Then in the second chapter called at a supposed Wedding of Cana, in Aramaic "Cana" means "the Disavowal" or negation, so it meant "The Disavowal" or Repudiation of Marriage, in Sacred Union with the Essene Vows of Continence or celibacy. Thus, the theology of Thomas Aquinas is riddled with error, altho parts are excellent, due to the ordinary basis being still the Old Testament tribal God, Yahweh of the Jews. This Yahweh led man into murder in conflicts and war, in the tradition of Cain and Abel, as well to sacrificed animals at an altar, justifying the eating of animal flesh, as well as bread eating. Thus, John based his Paradisian Essene Theology on the idea of "In the Beginning", while the <u>Word of God is the Conception of God, which is Image and Likeness of God,</u> in which <u>androgynous man was conceived in the beginning, (Gen.1:27)</u> or the ideal <u>Heavenly man whose Son comes on the clouds of Heaven.</u> This is John's "Father".

Now, after man sinned, both in sorrow and pain woman's conceptions were multiplied (Gen.3:16), so no longer unique in God's Conception, or the Communion in Spiritual Oneness, man is conceived by the oneness of the flesh in carnal sin, while man must labor in the sweat of his face for baked bread, and in the consequent acid-forming, desire wine and even flesh in unbalanced extreme foods, in a vicious syndrome that began in the violation of the Law of Life first given unto man, which the original Nazarite Essene vows sought to prevent. As to "the Word became flesh", in Aramaic it meant "the Word was realized by flesh," which Thomas Aquinas says meant "the Lord assumed flesh and dwelt among men", but this is true of spiritual assumption and conception also. As to the "Incarnation", "Fire, hail, snow, ice and stormy winds fulfill his Word" (Psalms 148:8), and "By the Word of God the heavens were established" (Psalms 32:6). As Thomas says: "The Word conceived by the Intellect is the Image or Exemplar of the thing understood", and "He is not called the Son of God as in excellence of nature, however great, but as one begotten of God's substance."

The Ascensional Science of Fruitarian Dietetics

Thomas also admits: "By reason of creation the name of divine sonship is suitable, for it belongs to all angels and saints." However, John calls him "the Only Begotten of the Father." (Jn.1:14) this means that the Word of God, and the Only Begotten son is begotten of God's substance, or Spirit, and not its opposite which is matter or the flesh.

Heaven, hail and stormy wind, angels and saints, all manifest or fulfill his Word, but the Only Begotten Son is necessarily Spirit like the Father in substance. This shows the truth of when the Essene Healer or Saviour says "This is my blood" of grape juice, the fruit of the vine, and "This is my body", of Saint John's Bread or carob and banana cakes, since in Holy Spirit God manifests what he conceives to be ideal in his creation. The Spirit (Wind, Breath) prevails (blows, breathes) where it pleases, and you hear its sound, but you do not know whence it come and whither it goes, such is every person who is born of God." (Jn.3:8) Flavius Josephus also said John was bereft of human nature, like a spirit without a body, so among men he was the Exemplar, the Hypostasis or Person of the son of God, but not fully ascended until he was Emptied or Void in the Ascension, which the Buddhists call Sunyata in Nirvana.

From this we see why, even if Simon the Zealot of the anti Cyrenian riots repented before succumbing on the cross in a drunken alcoholic stupor, he in no way died for us for our salvation, since the resurrection was no miracle, and many men have lived after being nailed to a cross losing blood. If any man resurrected, it was Simon of Bethany, who after being 4 days in a death-like trance of Divine Rapture returned to life.

John the Evangelist is the only one qualified as the Divine or True Theologian. Altho Jesus, the Sons the Living God, who John speaks about, seemingly travelled all over Palestine being present in Omnipresent Spirit, he was not incarnate as an individual in human flesh, altho he was present in the blood of the grape and in the flesh or rather substance of juicy fruits as a "palatable Jesus". Blood in Aramaic has identical meaning to likeness or image, while flesh means also despicable. The Gnostic Essene Mani thus wrote that a "palatable Jesus hung from every fruit tree", which St. Augustine learned being a Manichean until deluded by the Roman clergy. The only foundation the <u>Roman Papal Church stood upon</u> was the <u>persecution</u> of the Primitive Gnostics and the Inquisition, using <u>fear instead of faith</u> for conversion, thru the sinful slaughter of heretics, truly the blood-shed that perpetuated the Papal Church.

The Ascensional Science of Fruitarian Dietetics

Paul's doctrine that "God made his own Son in the likeness of sinful flesh", (Rom.8:3) shows Paul and the Roman Church supporters, are in error, with all their claims of "putting on the Christ" and Christ in their presence, as if mere faith was superior or sufficient in itself, not needing works or practice. Paul was a fish net maker, symbolically a snare for <u>"Fish"</u> or Christian converts, since Simon was told to become a fisher of men, and the miracle of "loaves and fishes" was with 2 fishes or converts who accompanied Jesus distributing the fig loaves. His defense of marriage, wine bibbing and flesh eating was diametrically contrary to the Paradisian Essene Ecclesia. From the murder of Stephen on thru his whole life he persecuted the Essenes, and only escaped trial in Jerusalem as a Roman henchman so as to be sent to Rome for his execution. He admittedly opposed Essenes calling them "false brethern", and Simon, Silvanus, and others were sent to spy out the freedom he pretended to have living like unbelievers.

    John says: "He who eats my body, and drinks my blood, has Life Everlasting and I shall raise him up in the last day" (Jn.6:54) showing <u>salvation comes by what we eat and drink,</u> and not by mere faith, nor even by Incarnation in sinful flesh. The sinful flesh can never rise up or ascend to Heaven. The Spiritualizing Fruitarian Dietetics is aimed at freeing man from sinful dense flesh for the etherealized Spiritualized Omnipresence in Heaven thru our Ascensional Science. As to being an Apostle, the Aramaic word means one "Sent by God", called or chosen so as to be authorized since they have realized perfect Oneness or Communion or Perfection like the Heavenly Father is Perfect. (Mt.5:48) thus, Mark 1:14 states: "After John attained Perfection, Jesus appeared in Galilee," which is mistranslated to mean "After John was delivered up" or imprisoned. But Herod who admired and protected him said, "John the Baptist has risen up from mortality, this is why miracles are worked by him", considering him the headmost prophet. (6:14) Thus we see like John living in the Presence of Christ or Apostle Beloved of Christ, his Apostles are the Elect, <u>set apart</u> or <u>perfected in discipline</u> having <u>subdued overcome carnal desires, fruitarian celibates</u> living like John on fruits in a frugal way of exemplary Perfection.

    "Change your way of life, because the Realm of the Intimate Presence is here." (Mt.3:2, 4:17) showing John was the oracle or speaker of the Word in the Wisdom of Jesus, the Invisible God no man has seen and those in the bosom (Presence) of the Father, declare him. (Jn.1:18) As for the Perfection in Jesus, John tells them, "I have appointed you that you should go and <u>produce fruit,</u> so your <u>fruit trees</u>

The Ascensional Science of Fruitarian Dietetics

remain..." (Jn.15:16) "That you may love one another." This is why the Lovewisdom Message has been "Build Paradises and eat the fruits thereof", because it inspires you to be love and enlighten others in Divine Wisdom. Now today we have a few doing this, but for the most part what the general Christians like Seventh Day Adventists get is a vegetarian diet, and one of the greatest obstacles and stumbling stones is the lack of a truly interpreted Fruitarian Gospel directly translated from Aramaic which only your author has realized in the "Buddhist Essene Gospel of Jesus". This is why he claims to have returned in the Spirit of John the original apostle beloved of Christ, beside having realized the Ascensional techniques or Way to Life Everlasting in heaven or Nirvana. This Grace comes from the Throne and Spirit of Grace which has to be earned by discipline.

WHY NOT AVOCADOS, OLIVES AND SEED OILS FOR SALADS?
Flavius Josephus recorded in "Jewish Antiquities" (Prologue): "They recoil from pleasure as something sinful: moderation and detachment from natural desires are virtues to them. They scorn to marry and adopt other people's children" as he describes the Essenes, and specially interesting to us now is that they eschew the use of oil and anointing the body: "OIL THEY CONSIDER IMPURE, IF ONE OF THEM HAS INADVERTENTLY BEEN IN CONTACT WITH OIL, HE MUST WASH HIS WHOLE BODY."

Your editor in his study of Syriac Aramaic and translating the Essene Allegories of John's Gospel, noted that Aramaic is a holy scriptural language, with the original Paradisian Essene doctrine built into it. For instance bread describes hostile, flesh condemns and is despicable, wine characterizes an ass, etc. thus, it is that BSA is a syllable used to write gladly, despise, make merry, condemn, ointment, unguent, anointing and flesh. So oil was despicable, defiling and condemned like flesh originally by the Essenes. There was no oil press in Eden and when the Apostles retired to Gethsemane, in our translation we suggested Simon the Zealot was hungry after the Fruit Supper of the Apostles, so as to eat the oil cakes discarded from the oil press, and thus mentally depressed denied he knew John the hypostasis of Jesus. It all goes back to the traitorous meaning of giving pleasure, defiling and condemning by the use of oil and anointing the flesh, likened to eating flesh.

The Ascensional Science of Fruitarian Dietetics

Likewise, the original American Hygienists condemned the use of salad oils, butterfat, etc. believing that if foods need to be greased to make them palatable and slide them down the gullet, they should not be eaten. Today, oils and avocados are a standby for most Hygienists if they don't use cottage cheese, nut butters, nuts or similar greasy or oily dressing for salads.

As we spoke quoting Rudolf Hauschka's words about "flower scents being etheric oils which contain hydrogen" which ascends, in turn he attributes "fatty oils" of seeds, plants grown for their oil content in fruit and seed, which certainly condemns the Avocados, Olives and Seed Oils. "The phenomenon takes place within the framework of the law of metamorphosis. The polar rhythm, expansion and contraction, being and appearance is its pattern. But what for the plant being is expansion and contraction, is just the opposite on the plane of appearance. Expansion, for the spirit, is material contraction, and vice versa. Thus, when the plant expands into the cosmos, its physical manifestation shrinks into the compass of the seed. The oil that forms the seeds under the influence of summer's heat is an inverse reflection of the plant's outstreaming. Cosmic fire in the sun's rays is condensed into oil, as it were concentrating forces of physical expansion in readiness for next spring's germination."

From the above hypothesis, we see that seeds, oily fruits and butterfat, are all gravitational forces seeking to bury humans who eat them. The animals need four legs to uplift them from earth's gravity, but man and the gods "little lower than angels", as Apollo describes Jesus were given dominion walking on two legs and with spiritual development they may ascend or levitate heavenwise in spirit free of the dross weight humans accumulate in gravitational substances. Heavy fat people accomplish little in their lives due to their difficulty to get around, and who ever heard of a fat aerialist, "floating thru the air with the greatest of ease, like the man on the flying trapeze"? Voluptuous characteristics are attractive to passionate people, just as they are repugnant to spiritual aspirants, and so should fatty or oleogenic foods to the ascensionally minded. As to being anointed or facially painted with greasy substances this asphyxiates the organism, in its excretory functions breathing thru the pores, causing the deformity and aging of appearance rather than health. Remember the golden goddesses of Greek theatrical displays painted with gold paint enabling a statue facsimile to move, but after the performance died as a consequence? The honor and pleasure of being anointed are foolish whims of royalty that asphyxiate

The Ascensional Science of Fruitarian Dietetics

the spirit and madden the mind. Even worse are suffocating fatty foods that sensual folk eat which enables unappetizing victuals to slide down the gullet, like a greased hog at a county fair who no one can subdue.

These thoughts remind me of my first view of Quito as it was early in 1941. We secured immigration visas for Ecuador on a British steamship camouflaged to avoid German submarine attacks barely escaping world War II U.S. entry. So arriving in Quito in 1941 barefoot without funds on a steam locomotive train unable to speak Spanish, everyone directed me to the Ecuadorian Northamerican School teaching English. Happily it was run by James M. who had just married a young lady from Ambato, he was trying to adapt her to his raw food diet. At lunch time, he gave me a coconut bowl with raw wheat grain, and thus we took turns grinding wheat with an old wooden box coffee mill, and this meal we kneaded a couple of drops of olive oil and two drops of honey with a spoon and slowly chewed thoroughly. After this cup of dry wheat meal, he accompanied the emaciated writer suffering from amoebic dysentery to the San Blas bus station adjacent to a market. James was greatly amused by dirty country farm people selling food cooked such as corn, fava beans, etc. boiled in water without salt which they relished, eaten out of a piece of old newspaper torn to serve as a plate. And to his amazement I purchased some capuli cherries under such unhygienic conditions, which I ate sitting on a wooden frame bus when he said good-bye. In a short time later a Rosicrucian with a master K.H. Pr. O.M. Chenrezi Lind, idled by and seeing me eating capulis, at once sought to get me to join them at their Center in Quito. It was a fabulous intuitive occurrence in that this high Tibetan Tashi lama had been sent in the transference of the world's Spiritual Shrine to the High Equatorial Andes due to Tibetan, Buddhist, Apocalyptic Essene and Pyramid Prophecies.

However, after numerous years I chanced to met with James again in Quito. He was teaching at the American High School with a home adjacent, and invited for a fruitarian repast I went. His buxom bride now with several children, served me fruits, but now she heaped animal flesh in soup in his bowl, bread, etc. as he sheepishly murmured that he had to get back on raw food. Trying to adapt to eating raw hash like wheat meal with little oil or honey was just as feasible as his returning. Most the people who try fruit few months end up with a facsimile history, sheepishly murmuring that fruit is unsubstantial.

The Ascensional Science of Fruitarian Dietetics

Back in 1941, for one dollar you obtained 14 sucres but today one dollar brings 6,000 sucres, and the dollar and sucre purchase a fraction what they did when men did a day of heavy work ditch-digging for one dollar in U.S.A. In Ecuador then one could buy ten bananas for one sucre or 5 tomatoes or oranges, but today I get one stock of small Orito bananas (unfumigated) for 10,000 s., or 24 organic tomatoes. The bananas have fruit sugars and acids with levitational forces, tannic acid especially in the skin providing iron against anemia in the high rarified air of Quito while in the lowlands the carbohydrates cannot be oxidized due to heavy asphyxiating barometric pressure inhibiting Hemoglobin formation, calcification of bone, etc. showing that life giving breath being more vital than food for life. Tomatoes are not only rich in citric, malic and oxalic acids or levitational force, the iron has affinity for calcium, as well as iron rendering harmless the cyanide-like poisons produced by the digestive processes. These are some of the foods organically produced around the Pifo region on the opposite side of the valley east of Quito, the high Andes protected Propitiatory Shelter of our camp of Saints paradigm.

By the end of this year of 1999 on to 2002 especially grave worldwide changes are on their way. "In one hour these great riches are destroyed" (Apoc.18:16) and "the first heaven and first earth had passed away, and I saw a new heaven and a new earth" (21:1) and "there fell a star from heaven, burning like a torch...and by these 3 plagues the third part of mankind are slain, by fire, by suffocation and sulfurous brimstone (8:10;9:18); they ascended to heaven in a cloud. (11:12) Come out of (Babylon) and be not smitten by her plagues, plagues shall come in one day, death, mourning and famine and she shall be burned with fire, for in one hour these great riches come to naught (18:4,8,16) they went up on the breadth (equator) and compassed the Camp of Saints, and fire came down out of heaven and devoured them." (20:9) This is confirmed by Apollo (Heb.12:26) "Foundation of earth shall shake, and reel to and fro like a drunkard." (Isaiah 25:18-20), Zacharias and others repeat the same prophecy of famine, economic crash, Cassini projectile burns like a meteor, nuclear fire rain and change of earth's axis, Camp of Saints survival. Excavations in Siberia show tropical animals and vegetation being once near the equator.

THE ASCENSIONAL SCIENCE OF SPIRITUALIZING FRUITARIAN DIETETICS
by Dr. Johnny Lovewisdom

After 25 million readers of the American weekly were informed he had been chosen as the Father of the New Race in 1942, in 1949 Doctor Johnny Lovewisdom was given renown described as a "Hermit" or "Saint of the Andes" to 100 million world-wide by the "Mundial" magazine of Montevideo "Picture Post" (G.B.) "Se" (Sweden) and numerous others in Europe.

"Only with the advent of the Paradisian New Race God-Born shall worth in my work be seen" Today 50 years later he continues as a Paradisian Essene still writing as a scientist about the Ascensional Science, and "Camp of Saints", after guiding top scientists to a "Sacred Valley of Longevity" at Vilcabamba, Ecuador and being viewed on T.V. since the 1960's. As disciplinarian, he warns the world of Apocalyptic disasters starting before the end of 1999 and the New Age.

"IT IS THE SPIRIT THAT GIVES LIFE; THE BODY PROFITS NOTHING; THE WORDS WHICH I HAVE SPOKEN TO YOU ARE SPIRIT AND LIFE. BUT THERE ARE SOME OF YOU WHO DO NOT BELIEVE. I HAVE TOLD YOU THAT NO MAN CAN COME TO ME UNLESS IT IS GIVEN TO HIM BY MY FATHER."
(John 6:63-65)

The Ascensional Science of Fruitarian Dietetics

THE DIET OF JOHN

Josephus, the renown historian who lived during the first century, says John lived on carob, eating neither bread of any kind nor the flesh of animals, beside refusing wine and intoxicating beverages. But the Gospels now read he ate "locusts and wild honey." The Locust tree and fruit are carob, otherwise known as "St. John's Bread" or food, because Luke (7:33) says he ate no bread. However, the words "wild honey" the Hebrew scholars in the Soncino Chumash translate as "fruits that exude sweet juices", such as "dates and figs". This would also include the sweet grape which yields a delicious juice when freshly pressed. In the sub-tropical Holy Land many sweet fruits abound including grape, fig, dates, banana, carob, cherimoya, mango, peach, apricot, plum, melon and citrus.

After experimenting with a fruit only diet Dr. Lovewisdom found it unworkable in practice and therefore returned to the Vitalogical Hygiene diet of fresh fruits, vegetables and grass-fed milk products like cheese and yogurt. A strict fruit diet can cause severe tooth damage in the long run and also hypoglycemia, hypothyroidism, fatigue and muscle mass loss, so kindly take heed and always include grass-fed dairy products and vegetables in your diet.

The Essene Gospel of Peace (originally titled The Essene Gospel of John), The Healing God Spell of Saint John and El Evangelio de la Salud (the spanish version of The Healing God Spell of Saint John) all concur that John included vegetables like lettuce, kale, celery, spinach, red cabbage, kohlrabi, tomatoes, cucumbers and herbs like basil and grasses like wheatgrass juice in addition to kindly treated, pasture raised milk products like yogurt and cheese. A gradual detoxification or transition diet is recommended to avoid overtaxing the body's eliminative organs.

Made in the USA
Monee, IL
16 April 2023

31960389R00052